CHAMONIX TO ZERMATT

About the Author

Kev Reynolds first visited the Alps in the 1960s, and returned there on numerous occasions to walk, trek or climb, to lead mountain holidays, devise multi-day routes or to research a series of guidebooks covering the whole range. A freelance travel writer and lecturer, he has a long association with Cicerone Press which began with his first guidebook to *Walks and Climbs in the Pyrenees*. Published in 1978 it has grown through many editions and is still in print. He has also written more than a dozen books on Europe's premier mountain range, a series of trekking guides to Nepal, a memoir covering some of his Himalayan journeys (*Abode of the Gods*) and a collection of short stories and anecdotes harvested from his 50 years of mountain activity (*A Walk in the Clouds*).

Kev is a member of the Alpine Club and Austrian Alpine Club. He was made an honorary life member of the Outdoor Writers and Photographers Guild; SELVA (the Société d'Etudes de la Littérature de Voyage Anglophone), and the British Association of International Mountain Leaders (BAIML). After a lifetime's activity, his enthusiasm for the countryside in general, and mountains in particular, remains undiminished, and during the winter months he regularly travels throughout Britain and abroad to share that enthusiasm through his lectures. Check him out on www.kevreynolds.co.uk

Other Cicerone guides by the author

CHAMONIX TO ZERMATT

THE CLASSIC WALKER'S HAUTE ROUTE

by Kev Reynolds

JUNIPER HOUSE, MURLEY MOSS,
OXENHOLME ROAD, KENDAL, CUMBRIA LA9 7RL
www.cicerone.co.uk

© Kev Reynolds 2019
Sixth edition 2019
ISBN: 978 1 78631 048 4

Fifth edition 2015
Fourth edition 2007
Third edition 2001
Second edition 1995
First edition 1991

Printed in China on behalf of Latitude Press Ltd
A catalogue record for this book is available from the British Library.
All photographs are by Kev Reynolds and Jonathan Williams unless otherwise stated.

Route mapping by Lovell Johns www.lovelljohns.com
Contains OpenStreetMap.org data © OpenStreetMap
contributors, CC-BY-SA. NASA relief data courtesy of ESRI

*For my wife – without whose love and practical support
this guidebook would not have been written.*

Updates to this Guide

While every effort is made by our authors to ensure the accuracy of guidebooks as they go to print, changes can occur during the lifetime of an edition. Any updates that we know of for this guide will be on the Cicerone website (www.cicerone. co.uk/1048/updates), so please check before planning your trip. We also advise that you check information about such things as transport, accommodation and shops locally. Even rights of way can be altered over time. We are always grateful for information about any discrepancies between a guidebook and the facts on the ground, sent by email to updates@cicerone.co.uk or by post to Cicerone, Juniper House, Murley Moss, Oxenholme Road, Kendal, LA9 7RL.

Register your book: To sign up to receive free updates, special offers and GPX files where available, register your book at www.cicerone.co.uk.

Front cover: Trekkers on the last part of the Europaweg beginning the gradual descent into Zermatt (Stage 14)

CONTENTS

Acknowledgements for 2019 edition

Research for this latest edition was undertaken by Jonathan, Lesley and Madeline Williams who not only acted as my legs and lungs but took over a thousand photos (a small selection of which grace this book) and supplied all the information to bring the guide up to date. I am profoundly grateful to each one of them. The Cicerone team at Juniper House transformed the words, photographs, maps and profiles into the attractive book you hold in your hands which, I trust, will enable you to enjoy the trek of a lifetime. I offer my thanks to them all, as ever, for enabling me to benefit from their talents and their friendship.

Mountain safety

Every mountain walk has its dangers, and those described in this guidebook are no exception. All who walk or climb in the mountains should recognise this and take responsibility for themselves and their companions along the way. The author and publisher have made every effort to ensure that the information contained in this guide was correct when it went to press, but, except for any liability that cannot be excluded by law, they cannot accept responsibility for any loss, injury or inconvenience sustained by any person using this book.

International distress signal *(emergency only)*
Six blasts on a whistle (and flashes with a torch after dark) spaced evenly for one minute, followed by a minute's pause. Repeat until an answer is received. The response is three signals per minute followed by a minute's pause.

Helicopter rescue
The following signals are used to communicate with a helicopter:

Help needed:
raise both arms
above head to
form a 'Y'

Help not needed:
raise one arm
above head, extend
other arm downward

Emergency telephone numbers
If telephoning from the UK the dialling codes are:
France: 0033; Switzerland: 0041

France: PGHM (Peloton de Gendarmerie de Haute Montagne):
tel 04 50 53 16 89; Emergency services: tel 112 (mobile phones)
Switzerland: OCVS (Organisation Cantonale Valaisanne de Secours): tel 144

Weather reports
France: Chamonix: tel 08 92 68 02 74, www.meteo.fr or tel 3250
Switzerland: tel 162 (in French, German or Italian), www.meteoschweiz.ch/en

Mountain rescue can be very expensive – be adequately insured.

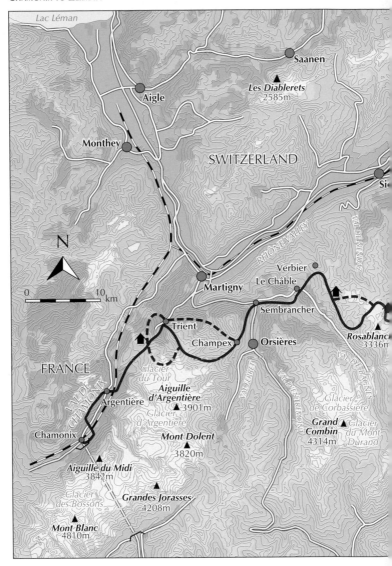

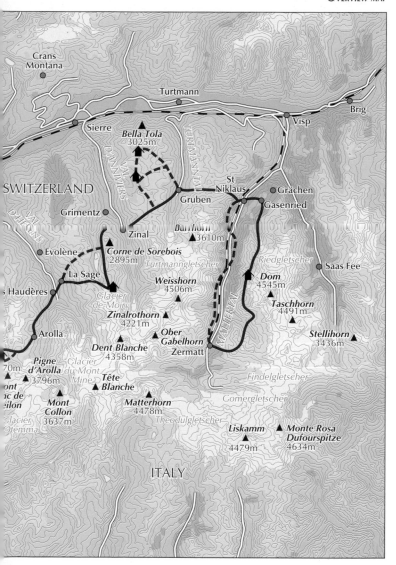

Looking across the Mattertal to the Weisshorn from the Europaweg (Stage 13)

Symbols used on route maps

~	route
- - -	alternative route
Ⓢ	start point
Ⓕ	finish point
Ⓢ	alternative start point
Ⓕ	alternative finish point
	glacier
	woodland
	urban areas
	regional border
	international border
━■━	station/railway
▲	peak
⬆ ⬆	manned/unmanned refuge
■	building
♁ ♁ †	church/monastery/cross
⌣	pass
•	water feature
•	other feature

Relief
in metres

4600–4800
4400–4600
4200–4400
4000–4200
3800–4000
3600–3800
3400–3600
3200–3400
3000–3200
2800–3000
2600–2800
2400–2600
2200–2400
2000–2200
1800–2000
1600–1800
1400–1600
1200–1400
1000–1200
800–1000
600–800
400–600
200–400
0–200

SCALE: 1:50,000

0 kilometres 0.5   1

0 miles   0.5

Contour lines are drawn at 25m intervals and highlighted at 100m intervals.

GPX files for all routes can be downloaded free at www.cicerone.co.uk/1048/GPX.

ROUTE SUMMARY TABLE

Stage no.	Start/Finish	Distance (km)	Time (hr:min)	Ascent (m)	Descent (m)	Page
1	Chamonix – Argentière	9	2:15	300	85	48
2	Argentière – Trient	15	5:30	1000	975	56
3	Trient – Champex	16	7:00	1390	1200	69
4	Champex – Le Châble	14.5	4:15	200	840	83
5	Le Châble – Cabane du Mont Fort	13	5:30	1660	20	92
6	Cabane du Mont Fort – Cabane de Prafleuri	17	7:30	1110	940	104
7	Cabane de Prafleuri – Arolla	18	6:00	740	1360	116
8	Arolla – La Sage	11.5	4:00	520	860	130
9	La Sage – Cabane de Moiry	15	6:00	1680	520	139
10	Cabane de Moiry – Zinal	19.5	7:00	650	1800	155
11	Zinal – Gruben	17	6:00	1250	1100	166
12	Gruben – St Niklaus	18	7:00	1150	1850	189
12A	St Niklaus – Gasenried	4	2:00	600	70	203
13	Gasenried – Europa Hut	15	6:30	1180	570	208
14	Europa Hut – Zermatt	23	7:00	850	1510	216
Total		**225.5**	**83.30**	**14,280**	**13,700**	

Stage no.	Start/Finish	Distance (km)	Time (hr:min)	Ascent (m)	Descent (m)	Page
Alternative stages						
3A	Trient – Champex	16	5:45	1040	850	77
5A	Le Châble (Les Ruinettes) – Cabane de Louvie	10	4:00	640	600	101
9A	La Sage – Barrage de Moiry	13	5:00	1250	670	147
10A	Barrage de Moiry – Zinal	9	4:00	600	1170	161
11A	Zinal – Hôtel Weisshorn	11	3:30	810	150	174
11B	Hôtel Weisshorn – Gruben	11	4:00	600	1120	181
13A/ 14A	St Niklaus – Zermatt	23	5:30	720	240	226

Facilities symbols

🛈	information centre	🚉	train station
◯	hotel/B&B/accommodation	🚌	bus service
🍴	café/restaurant/food	🚠	cable car
🛒	shop/groceries	▲	manned hut
🏧	ATM/bank	△	unmanned hut

The Matterhorn and the Stellisee above Zermatt

PREFACE TO THE SIXTH EDITION

Since the first edition of this guide was published in 1991, the Walker's Haute Route between Chamonix and Zermatt has become accepted as one of the finest of all Alpine treks, growing in popularity among both individual and group trekkers from around the world. It's not difficult to see why. The scenery is second to none, trails are clearly defined almost everywhere, the passes offer both challenge and reward in equal measure, and accommodation is plentiful and varied. It is little wonder that some trekkers return more than once to enjoy this classic route and introduce others to its delights.

But the Alpine landscape changes year by year – often in dramatic fashion through rockfall, avalanche or flood. Snowfields shrink, moraines crumble, glaciers withdraw and even disappear completely. Nowhere is immune to change, and that is certainly true of the region through which this trek makes its way. This latest edition of the guide reflects changes that have occurred since the previous updated edition was published. In some cases the way has been rerouted, improved, safeguarded or provided with better waymarking. On some stages new signage indicates the adoption of the route by the Swiss National Walking Route 6, and on the final stage of the trek, the world's longest pedestrian suspension bridge has been created on the exciting Europaweg above the Mattertal.

All these changes were noted on my behalf by Jonathan, Lesley and Madeline Williams during their research trek in the summer of 2018, and I am deeply indebted to them for their attention to detail. They also recorded the distances covered on each stage, as well as height gained and lost, with a greater degree of accuracy than I had for previous editions. All of which should both aid in the planning of your trek and when you set out with this guidebook in hand on what is an epic and exquisitely scenic journey from Mont Blanc to the Matterhorn.

May you find your trek along this route to be as enriching and rewarding as each one of mine has been.

Kev Reynolds

The Grand Combin, seen from the path between the Col Termin and the Col de Louvie (Stage 6)

INTRODUCTION

Coming in to Arolla, more a hamlet than a village but with most services the trekker could desire (Stage 7)

Chamonix to Zermatt, Mont Blanc to the Matterhorn. What pictures these names conjure in the minds of those of us who love mountains! The two greatest mountaineering centres in the world – one overshadowed by the highest massif in Western Europe and the other by the most famous, if not the most elegant and most instantly recognised, of all mountains.

Chamonix to Zermatt, Mont Blanc to the Matterhorn – a recipe for a visual feast!

To walk from one to the other is to sample that feast in full measure; a gourmet extravaganza of scenic wonders from first day till last, and each one (to carry the metaphor to its limit) a course that both satisfies and teases the palate for more. The Walker's Haute Route does just that.

In two weeks of mountain travel you will be witness to the greatest collection of 4000m peaks in all the Alps and visit some of the most spectacular valleys. There you'll find delightful villages and remote alp hamlets, wander flower meadows and deep fragrant forests, skirt exquisite tarns that toss mountains on their heads, cross icy streams and clamber beside glaciers that hang suspended from huge buttresses of rock. You'll traverse lonely passes and descend into wild, stone-filled corries. There will be marmots among the boulders and ibex on the heights. And your days will be filled with wonder.

It's more demanding than the well-known Tour of Mont Blanc, for the route is over 225km long; it crosses 11 passes, gains and loses close to 14,000m in height. But each pass gained is a window onto a world of stunning beauty.

There's the Mont Blanc range and the chain of the Pennine Alps, one massif after another of snow-bound glory: Mont Blanc itself, with its organ-pipe aiguilles; the overpowering mass of the Grand Combin; Mont Blanc de Cheilon and Pigne d'Arolla, Mont Collon and Tête Blanche and the huge tooth of Dent Blanche. There's the Grand Cornier, Ober Gabelhorn and Weisshorn and stiletto-pointed Zinalrothorn; then there's the Dom and Täschhorn, Breithorn and Matterhorn and all their crowding neighbours sheathed in ice and snow to act as a backcloth

to dreams; a background landscape to the Walker's Haute Route, contender for the title of Most Beautiful Walk in Europe.

THE WALKER'S HAUTE ROUTE

The original High Level Route (*Haute Route*), from Chamonix to Zermatt and beyond, was developed more than a hundred years ago. But this was very much a mountaineer's expedition, for it traced a meandering line among the great peaks of the Pennine Alps by linking a number of glacier passes. James David Forbes, scientist and active mountaineer, pioneered an important section of this in 1842 when he crossed Col d'Hérens, Col de Fenêtre and Col du Mont Collon. Alfred Wills also made early explorations, but it was mainly a joint effort by other members of the Alpine Club,

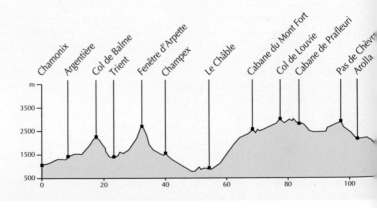

notably JF Hardy, William Mathews, Francis Fox Tuckett, FW Jacomb and Stephen Winkworth and their guides, that saw a complete High Level Route established in 1861. This route went from Chamonix to Col d'Argentière, then via Val Ferret, Orsières, Bourg St Pierre, Col de Sonadon, Col d'Oren, Praraye, Col de Valpelline and on to Zermatt.

The following year (1862) Col des Planards was discovered, which led to Orsières being bypassed, thereby allowing a better line to be made in the link between the northern edge of the Mont Blanc range and that of the Pennine Alps.

This High Level Route was, of course, primarily a summer mountaineering expedition that was no small undertaking, especially when one considers the fact that at the time there were no mountain huts

as we know them now and all supplies had to be carried a very long way. But with the introduction of skis to the Alps in the late 19th century a new concept in winter travel became apparent, and with the first important ski tour being made in the Bernese Alps in 1897, and the subsequent winter ascent of major mountains aided by ski (Monte Rosa in 1898, Breithorn 1899, Strahlhorn 1901, etc), it was clearly only a matter of time before the challenge of the High Level Route would be subjected to winter assault.

In 1903 the first attempt was made to create a ski traverse of the Pennine Alps, and although this and other attempts failed, in January 1911 Roget, Kurz, Murisier, the brothers Crettex and Louis Theytaz succeeded in establishing a winter route from Bourg St Pierre to Zermatt.

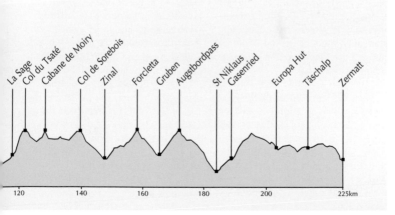

From the Col de Prafleuri, the Col des Roux and mountains above Arolla are clearly visible (Stage 6)

Having successfully hijacked the original High Level Route as the ski-touring route par excellence, and having translated its British title as the Haute Route, the journey from Chamonix to Zermatt came to be seen almost universally as a winter (or more properly, a spring) expedition; a true classic that is, understandably, the focus of ambition for many experienced skiers and ski-mountaineers today.

But there's another Chamonix to Zermatt high-level route that is very much a classic of its kind; a walker's route that never quite reaches 3000m on any of its passes, that requires no technical mountaineering skills to achieve, avoids glacier crossings and yet rewards with some of the most dramatic high mountain views imaginable.

This is the Chamonix to Zermatt Walker's Haute Route.

It leads comfortably from the base of Mont Blanc to the Swiss frontier at Col de Balme, and from there down to Trient following the route of the Tour of Mont Blanc or one of its variants (*variantes*). The next pass is Fenêtre d'Arpette leading to Champex, and from there down to the junction of Val d'Entremont and Val de Bagnes, then curving round the foot of the mountains to Le Châble. Avoiding Verbier, a steep climb brings you to Cabane du Mont Fort, and continues high above the valley heading south-east before crossing three cols in quick succession in order to pass round the northern flanks of Rosablanche.

From Cabane de Prafleuri the route heads over Col des Roux and along the shores of Lac des Dix, then on to Arolla by one of two ways: Col de Riedmatten or the neighbouring Pas de Chèvres via Cabane des Dix. Arolla leads to Les Haudères and up to La Sage on a green hillside above Val d'Hérens in readiness for tackling either Col de Torrent or Col du Tsaté. Both these cols give access to Val de Moiry and its hut perched in full view of a tremendous icefall, from where the crossing of Col de Sorebois takes the walker into Val de Zinal, the upper reaches of the glorious Val d'Anniviers. From Zinal to Gruben in the Turtmanntal the route once again has two options to consider: either by way of Hôtel Weisshorn or Cabane Bella Tola and the Meidpass, or by the more direct Forcletta. After leaving Gruben a final climb to the ancient crossing point of the Augstbordpass leads to the Mattertal. The final stage adopts the dramatic Europaweg, a true high-level traverse of the east wall of the valley, with an overnight stay in the Europa Hut and a crossing of the new 500-metre Charles Kuonen bridge across an area of unstable mountain and gorge, before the Matterhorn finally comes into full view on the final descent into Zermatt. An alternative valley route is possible if the high route is closed, time doesn't allow or the exposed and cabled route and the thought of the bridge (actually rather wonderful) doesn't appeal.

Every stage has its own special attributes, its own unique splendour, and all add up to a walk of classic proportions. It is, of course, a scenic extravaganza whose main features

A glimpse of the Grand Combin from near the Col de la Chaux (Stage 6, photo: Madeline Williams)

are the mountains that form the landscapes through which you walk.

First of these is dominated by the Mont Blanc massif with its towering aiguilles creating stark outlines against a backwash of snow and ice. Unbelievably high and seemingly remote from valley-based existence, the dome of the Monarch of the Alps glows in evening light, shines under a midday sun and imposes itself on panoramas viewed from cols several days' walk from the crowded boulevards of Chamonix.

Then there's the Grand Combin making a fair imitation of its loftier neighbour as it soars above the deeply cut Val de Bagnes. This too is a vast mountain whose presence is felt many days' walk away, a grand block of glacial artistry that lures and entices from afar.

Heading round Rosablanche gives a taste of the other side of the mountain world, where gaunt screes and dying glaciers contrast the gleaming snows of its upper slopes. But then Mont Blanc de Cheilon returns the eye to grandeur on an epic scale, with Pigne d'Arolla and Mont Collon adding their handsome profiles for close inspection, while far off a first brief glimpse of the Matterhorn promises much for the future.

Walkers reaching the col at the Pas de Chèvres from the Arolla side (Stage 7)

Val de Moiry holds many surprises with its tarns, dammed lake, majestic icefall and contorted glaciers, while Col de Sorebois and all the way down to Zinal is one long adoration of the Weisshorn. The head of Val de Zinal is so magnificent that one yearns to be able to explore further, but the route northward denies that opportunity yet still allows it to be seen in true perspective – a fabulous cirque giving birth to glaciers that have carved a valley of much loveliness.

The Turtmanntal takes you back to the 19th century. Above it once more rises the Weisshorn, along with Tête de Milon, Bishorn and Brunegghorn and a caliper of glaciers spilling into the valley.

One of the finest viewpoints of the whole walk comes an hour and a half below the Augstbordpass between Turtmanntal and Mattertal. The Mattertal is a long green shaft 1000m below. Across the valley shines the Dom with the tongue-like Riedgletscher (glacier) hanging from it. Above to the right is the Brunegghorn with the Weisshorn beyond, while at the head of the valley is seen that great snowy mass which runs between Monte Rosa and the Matterhorn. But the Matterhorn itself keeps you waiting. Cross the valley at St Niklaus and climb steeply to Gasenried, then walk the length of the Europaweg and you'll not only have the Bishorn and Weisshorn (yet again), but also the Schalihorn, Pointe Sud de Moming and Zinalrothorn,

and the incomparable Matterhorn at last seen as it should be seen, from its roots above Zermatt to its cocked-head summit nearly 3000m above the valley. It's a view worth waiting for. A view worth walking all the way from Chamonix to savour.

Despite its high passes, despite the fact that it runs across the grain of the country where deep valleys slice between the long outstretched arms of some of the highest mountains in Western Europe, the Chamonix to Zermatt route is not the sole preserve of the hardened mountain walker – although there are some taxing stages and a few delicate exposed sections that might give an understandable twinge of concern to first-time wanderers among the Alps. Most days lead into a touch of 'civilisation', albeit sometimes this civilisation might be just a small mountain village with few amenities. Every night there will be a lodging place with the possibility of meals provided, thereby making it unnecessary to carry camping or cooking equipment. Backpacking on this route is a choice, not an obligation.

Lodgings on the Walker's Haute Route are in themselves very much a part of the mountain experience. In villages they allow you to capture some of the region's culture. In remote mountain huts the wanderer is introduced to the climber's world, with an opportunity to witness high alpine scenes that are normally privy only to the mountaineer.

The Weisshorn from the Europa Hut (Stages 13 and 14)

Accommodation varies from hotels (there are luxuriously appointed hotels in certain villages on the route for those inclined and financially able to make use of them), to gîtes and basic refuges, and mattresses spread on the floor of communal dormitories in the attic of a pension or inn. But those planning to camp must understand that organised campsites are not to be found in all valleys, and that wild camping is officially discouraged in Switzerland.

Wherever lodgings (and campsites) are to be found along the route mention is made in the text. Similarly, wherever alternative methods of transport occur (train, bus, cablecar, etc), brief details are given. This is to aid any walkers who might fall behind their schedule due to bad weather, unseasonal conditions, sickness or just plain weariness.

The walk outlined in this guide may be achieved within a two-week holiday, while those with plenty of time available are given options which would extend the route and increase the overall experience. These options are outlined below. The longest stage demands 7½ hours of walking, but there are several days of only 4 hours each. Some of the less demanding days could be amalgamated by fit trekkers in order to reduce the time required to complete the route, should they not have a full fortnight at their disposal, but it would be a pity to do so. This is a route that deserves to be wandered at a gentle pace; the very best of mountain holidays.

The first stage (Chamonix to Argentière – 2hr 15min) may be seen as a prelude. Should you arrive late in the day in Chamonix then you would probably only have sufficient time to reach Argentière on foot that day. However, if your travel arrangements get you to Chamonix at a reasonable time in the morning (on the overnight train from Paris, for example), it might be feasible to walk all the way to Trient, thus combining two stages for a 7½–8hr day, thereby cutting a day off the overall route allocation.

Stage 12A (St Niklaus to Gasenried) links the original Haute Route with the new finish along the Europaweg, and takes about 2hr walking time. However, it is not really practical to add this short stage to the demanding Augstbordpass crossing (Stage 12), nor to tack it on at the start of Stage 13. If you cannot allow a full day for this walk, it is possible to take a bus from St Niklaus to Gasenried itself – either at the end of Stage 12, or first thing on the morning of Stage 13.

Several commercial trekking companies follow a large portion of the Walker's Haute Route, but opt for public transport over some sections in order to allow a day or two in Zermatt at the end of a two-week holiday. This is an option available to the individual trekker too, of course. But again, it would be a shame to miss any single stage of this route, for each bears witness to the last and forms a unique link with the next.

The complete route: 14/15 days	
1	Chamonix – Argentière
2	Argentière – Col de Balme – Trient
3	Trient – Fenêtre d'Arpette – Champex
4	Champex – Sembrancher – Le Châble
5	Le Châble – Clambin – Cabane du Mont Fort
6	Cabane du Mont Fort – Cabane de Prafleuri
7	Cabane de Prafleuri – Arolla
8	Arolla – Les Haudères – La Sage
9	La Sage – Col du Tsaté – Cabane de Moiry
10	Cabane de Moiry – Col de Sorebois – Zinal
11	Zinal – Forcletta – Gruben
12	Gruben – Augstbordpass – St Niklaus
12A	St Niklaus – Gasenried
13	Gasenried – Europa Hut
14	Europa Hut – Zermatt

A 12-day trek	
1	Chamonix – Trient
2	Trient – Champex
3	Champex – Le Châble
4	Le Châble – Cabane du Mont Fort
5	Cabane du Mont Fort – Cabane de Prafleuri
6	Cabane de Prafleuri – Arolla
7	Arolla – La Sage
8	La Sage – Cabane de Moiry
9	Cabane de Moiry – Zinal
10	Zinal – Gruben
11	Gruben – St Niklaus
12	St Niklaus – Zermatt

GETTING THERE AND BACK AGAIN

Air travel to Switzerland is relatively inexpensive. There are regular scheduled flights from most countries in Europe, the US and other international start points. It is well served by low-cost airlines flying from the UK as well as other operators. Regular scheduled flights from the UK are operated principally by British Airways (www.britishairways.com), easyJet (www.easyjet.com) and Swiss International Airlines (www.swiss.com). Aer Lingus (www.aerlingus.ie) flies from Dublin.

Geneva is the most convenient airport for reaching Chamonix. British Airways currently flies there from London Heathrow and Gatwick, Birmingham and Manchester. Low-cost easyJet has regular services from Gatwick, Luton, East Midlands, Liverpool and Manchester while Swiss International Airlines operates out of London (Heathrow and City), Birmingham, Manchester and Edinburgh. Aer Lingus has an infrequent service from Dublin.

On arrival at Geneva **onward travel to Chamonix** is either by road or rail. For all road options visit www.chamonix.net/english/transport. Options include a twice-daily bus from the airport by the French-operated SAT Autocar (tel 04 50 78 05 33), by minibus (www.mountaindropoffs.com, www.chamvan.com and others), or by train from the airport to Martigny, where you

change to the Mont Blanc Express (change again at Le Châtelard on the Swiss/French border). On balance, the convenience and cost of the Airport–Chamonix minibuses is the most straightforward, but reserve in advance.

Travel by rail is straightforward. A superfast London–Paris service is operated by Eurostar through the Channel Tunnel, with onward journey to Chamonix. For up-to-date rail information contact Rail Europe (www.raileurope.com) or visit (www.thetrainline.com).

Return from Zermatt at the end of the walk will be by train via Visp to Geneva (for flight), or to Lausanne (connections for Paris-bound trains).

If you don't have reservations from Geneva and are returning by plane, there are probably more and better connections from Zurich airport (reached by train in 3 to 4 hours).

ACCOMMODATION

Practically every village along the route of this walk has a wide selection of accommodation and facilities to choose from, while between villages there are often mountain inns of one sort or another where an overnight lodging may be found. In the early stages there are also several **gîtes d'étape** which are very much like privately owned youth hostels, with (usually) low-cost dormitory accommodation and communal washrooms. In addition, there are privately owned

The inviting Hôtel du Glacier in Arolla (Stage 7)

mountain huts and others belonging to the Swiss Alpine Club in which non-members can spend a night too.

Outline details are given throughout the text wherever lodgings exist. Telephone numbers are also provided where possible to enable walkers to call ahead to reserve beds – this is especially important during the high season.

It might also be worth noting that the cost of accommodation in Switzerland need not be as prohibitively high as some might fear. While it is pointless quoting specific prices in a guidebook that could be in print for several years, prices in Switzerland may feel high to UK and US visitors, although the exchange rate changes will determine how high. Hotel prices for half-board (*demi-pension/ halb-pension*) with the standard meal can be the most reasonable, but à la carte dining can become expensive. Hotel standards are high, and service will be friendly.

In a few villages along the way it may be possible to rent a private room in a furnished chalet for a night. Some of these rooms have self-catering facilities, otherwise you will need to find a restaurant for your meals. A self-contained room can be economically viable, and where such places are known from personal experience, mention is made in the text. Otherwise, enquire at the local tourist office.

Dortoirs (*matratzenlager* or *massenlager* in German) are recommended for walkers who do not object to a lack of privacy. Some hotels offer dortoir accommodation in an attic or an outbuilding, while a few establishments are specifically set up as privately run youth hostels – the *gîtes d'étape* mentioned above. In my experience these places offer good value for money. They vary in style, but all provide mixed dormitory accommodation and simple washing facilities and hot showers. Some have individual two-tier bunk beds, others merely offer mattresses on the floor of a large room under the roof. One or two also provide the means for self-catering, while the majority offer a full meals service. Those with experience of staying in youth hostels should be more than content with the dortoirs on the Chamonix to Zermatt route.

Mountain huts of the Swiss Alpine Club (SAC) are also used on this route – as well as some that are privately owned. Membership of an affiliated alpine club with reciprocal rights will give reduced overnight fees in SAC huts. (If you are a member of the UK section of the Austrian Alpine Club, for example, or the Swiss Alpine Club do not forget to take your membership card with you.) Members of the British Mountaineering Council (BMC) can also obtain a reciprocal rights card that is recognised here. (Addresses and contact numbers of both the Austrian Alpine Club and BMC will be found in Appendix C.)

Mountain huts have mixed dormitory accommodation. Most of those visited on this route provide meals and drinks (neither Refuge Les Grands on Stage 2, alternative finish, nor Refuge de la Gentiane la Barma passed on Stage 7, is permanently manned in summer). Evening meals in huts are invariably filling and high in calorific value, but washroom facilities are sometimes rather basic, although a shower is nearly always available. Sometimes water supply in the high mountain huts can be limited, but this is not usually the case.

As for camping, officially approved sites are to be found in a number of valleys along the route, but certainly not in all of them. Where they do exist facilities range from adequate to good. Off-site camping is officially discouraged in Switzerland since grasslands form a valuable part of the agricultural economy, and although it would not be beyond the bounds of possibility for individual backpackers to find a discreet corner of an alp for a single night's stay, it would be irresponsible to indicate likely sites in this book. Wherever possible please ask permission of farmers. It has always been my experience in Switzerland that whenever a farmer has been approached, permission has readily been granted and a good site pointed out. In all cases, wherever you camp be discreet, take care not to foul water supplies, light no fires and pack all litter away with you.

Mention of any establishment in this book, whether as an overnight lodging or as a place where refreshments may be had, should not necessarily be taken as an endorsement of services on offer.

HUT ETIQUETTE

On arrival at a mountain hut remove your boots before entering and help yourself to a pair of hut shoes found on a rack just inside the door. Locate the guardian to book bedspace for the night and put your name down for any meals you may require. There will sometimes be a choice of menu, but not always. It is usually possible to order a packed lunch or sandwich for the following day. Blankets and pillows are provided in the dormitories, but you need to bring a sleeping bag liner with you for purposes of hygiene, indeed most huts insist on this. Some of these huts are used by climbers who may need to make a pre-dawn start, and while your sleep may be disturbed by those leaving early, it is important that you do not disturb others if you go to bed after they have settled. Lights out is normally 10pm, if you last that long! Breakfast times vary but usually start at 6.30 or 7am.

WHEN TO GO

The best time to tackle any high-level trek in the Alps will be dictated by the amount and timing of the previous winter's snowfall and the onset of cold, inclement weather in the autumn. As the Walker's Haute Route crosses several high passes and negotiates some remote and difficult terrain where a lot of snow cover could create problems or even danger, it is not advisable in a 'normal' year to consider setting out before early July, although mountain huts are usually open from mid-June. During some years even that could be too soon, although one would normally expect most of the snow (and with it the risk of avalanche) to have gone by then, and flowers to be in full bloom. Hard névé can linger through a whole summer, especially after winters with heavy snow. But do bear in mind that it is not unusual for parts of the Alps to have a sudden dump of snow even in the middle of August. The only certainty when it comes to predicting alpine weather is that any long-range forecast is bound to be unpredictable!

A trek from mid-June onwards is certainly possible, but you should check snow conditions before departure and be equipped with ice-axe and crampons, and be ready to deal with mountaineering conditions in order to safely undertake the route.

In the high summer period of July to the middle of August, when the trails are at their busiest, temperatures can rise to 25–30°C even at altitudes of 2500m and more, and afternoon thunderstorms may be expected.

Autumn begins in mid-September, often bringing long periods of fine weather with clear skies by day and the first frosts at night. By the end of September most huts will close, except for a simple 'winter

29

Evening light over the Val d'Arpette and the Ecandies and Orny peaks (Stage 3)

room' which remains open with basic amenities. October can be magical when the larchwoods turn to gold and shrubs on the hillsides are ablaze with scarlet leaves. But heavy rain, and the first of winter's snow falling on the higher hills, can restrict high-altitude walking, or at least reduce its pleasure.

Perhaps the most favourable period to trek the Walker's Haute Route, from both a weather perspective and also for availability of accommodation, is from mid-August to the middle of September.

Day-to-day weather forecasts, in German, French or Italian, may be obtained in Switzerland by telephone (tel 62), while daily and five-day forecasts are available on www.meteoswiss.admin.ch or through its app (see 'Recommended apps'). Local tourist information offices and guides' bureaux often display a 2–3 day forecast, and sometimes there's a barometer on show by which you can check pressure trends. Up-to-date advice may also be sought from the guardians at mountain huts.

NOTES FOR WALKERS

Those who tackle the Chamonix to Zermatt route will reap countless rewards. And those rewards will be more easily gathered if you are physically fit and mentally attuned. Crossing the grain of the country means that there will be many steep uphill and downhill sections to face, and since it is important to enjoy every aspect of the first pass as much as the last, fitness should be there from the very beginning.

Taking regular exercise at home will go some way towards getting in condition for the physical demands of the route. Of course, the best way to prepare yourself for a mountain walking holiday is by walking. Uphill. Carry a rucksack with a few belongings in it to accustom your shoulders to the weight. If on the first day out from Chamonix your lungs and legs complain, then you have probably not done enough to get fit, and the crossing of Col de Balme will be less enjoyable than it deserves. In this case it may be advisable to take the lower Bovine route on Stage 3 rather than the more arduous Fenêtre d'Arpette.

Mental fitness is as important as the physical, and the two often go hand in hand. If you gaze with dread at the amount of height to be gained in order to cross a pass, no doubt you will suffer in consequence. Let every day be greeted with eagerness. Find joy in the steep uphill as well as the downward slope. Draw strength from the beauty of the scenes around you. Enjoy the movement of clouds, the wind and wildness as much as the gleam of sunshine; the raw crags and screes of desolation as well as the lush flower-strewn pastures and distant snowscapes. Each is an integral part of the mountain world; a world

of magic and mystery. It's a world through which it is a privilege to move in freedom. Don't take a moment of this experience for granted.

Since walking across mountains is thirsty work, you'll need to start each day with a full water bottle – at least 1 litre per person. And there's a good chance that you'll need to top up during the day too. On a number of stages there will be a water trough fed by a spring located near farm buildings or in a pasture. Filling your bottle from the feeder pipe should be perfectly safe. As for taking water directly from streams, in more than 40 years of trekking in the Alps, I've never had any problems from drinking from mountain streams as long as they're fast running and located above any grazing animals. But to be safe, it would be advisable to treat stream water with purification tablets or other filtration methods, available from pharmacies or specialist outdoor retailers.

NOT ENOUGH TIME?

As with many treks, the route is best savoured with ample time. But for those with less time there are options that take advantage of Switzerland's (and France's) public transport network.

- Stage 1 to Argentière can be combined with Stage 2 to Trient for a 7–8 hour day. There are bus and train options to Argentière and La Tour, as well as ski lifts towards the Col de Balme.

The fabulous Val de Zinal headwall seen from the trail to Hôtel Weisshorn (Stage 11A)

- There are cablecar options from Le Châble to Les Ruinettes, leaving a short walk to the Cabane du Mont Fort that can be fitted into Stage 4 from Champex to Le Châble. (There are also bus options between Champex and Le Châble.)
- Possible bus options between Arolla and La Sage.
- It is possible to fit Stages 9A and 10A between La Sage and the Moiry Barrage and then to Zinal in a single long day.
- Finish the trek at St Niklaus, or take the one-day valley route to Zermatt.

Alternatively, you could split the route at Arolla and return for the rest another year.

EQUIPMENT

As for clothing and equipment, what you choose to take will be crucial to your overall enjoyment of the trek.

- Boots need to be lightweight, comfortable, fit well and be broken in before leaving home. They should give ankle support and have thick cleated soles (Vibram or similar) with plenty of grip.
- Good waterproofs are essential, not just as protection from rain or snowfall, but to double as windproofs. Jacket and overtrousers made from a 'breathable' material are recommended. Bearing in mind that some of the passes are almost 3000m high, a warm fleece should also be taken, as should a warm hat or balaclava, and gloves.

- A lightweight collapsible umbrella can be indispensable on days of heavy rain for those who wear glasses.
- It is also necessary to take preventative action against long periods of extreme heat and unshaded sun. A brimmed sunhat, suncream (factor 30 or stronger) and sunglasses should be part of your equipment.
- A first-aid kit must be included (see under 'Safety in the mountains').
- Water bottle, compass, headtorch and spare batteries, whistle and maps should also be carried, as should a small amount of emergency food. (This can be replenished regularly as you pass through villages.)
- A sheet sleeping bag (sleeping bag liner) is highly recommended for use in dortoirs and mountain huts. A conventional sleeping bag, however, will not be needed unless you plan to camp.
- A lightweight towel and personal toiletry items (plus toilet paper and lighter).
- Trekking poles will ease the strain on legs and knees, especially on the many steep downhill sections.
- Bivvy bag (or space blanket) in case of emergencies.
- A comfortable rucksack with waist-belt adjusted to take the weight of your pack is important. You should be able to keep equipment down to 10kg (20lb)

at most – unless you plan to backpack with full camping gear.
- A waterproof cover for your pack is essential, plus stuffsacs or a large thick polythene bag so you can pack all your equipment inside the sack. Doing so should protect items from getting damp in the event of bad weather. A selection of plastic bags of assorted sizes will also be useful.
- In June or early July ice-axe and crampons may be necessary. Call huts or tourist offices to check.

LANGUAGES

On all but the final two valleys of the walk the route passes through French-speaking territory, but once you cross from Zinal into the Turtmanntal German becomes the official language. Although the non-linguist may have difficulty conversing in general terms with locals met in the mountains, English is widely understood in most of the villages, and you will face no real language problems in hotels or other lodgings. Appendix E contains a glossary of French and German words likely to be met along the way, but is no substitute for either a pocket dictionary, phrase-book or app.

PATHS AND WAYMARKS

Most of the paths adopted by this route will have been in use for centuries by farmers, traders and hunters going about their daily business

– from alp to alp, or from one valley to the next by way of an ancient pass. A few will be of recent origin, either laid out by a local commune, by a branch of the Swiss Footpath Protection Association, by the Valais Rambling Association (Association Valaisanne de la Randonnée Pédestre) or by members of the SAC in order to reach a mountain hut.

There are two official types of footpath in Switzerland which are signposted and waymarked to a common standard. A *chemin pedestre* (*wanderweg*) is a path that remains either in the valley or along the hillsides at a modest altitude. These are maintained and graded at a more gentle angle than the *chemin de montagne* or *bergweg*. Yellow metal signposts bear the names of major

Well-signed path junctions make navigation straightforward on most parts of the trail

landmark destinations such as a pass, lake, hut or village, often with estimated times given in hours (*heures* in French, *stunden* in German-speaking regions) and minutes (*min*). A plate on these yellow signs names the immediate locality and, sometimes, the altitude. Along the trail occasional yellow signs or paint flashes on rocks are also found.

A mountain path (*chemin de montagne* or *bergweg*) is one which ventures higher and is more demanding than the *chemin pedestre/wanderweg*. These paths will usually be rougher, narrower and steeper. Most are in regular use. Signposting will be similar to that already described, except that the outer sections of the finger post will be painted red and white, and the intermediate paint flashes along the way will be blazed white–red–white. Occasional cairns may also be used to direct the way over boulder slopes, or where poor visibility could create difficulties. In the event of mist or low cloud obscuring the onward route, it is essential to study the area of visibility with the utmost care before venturing on to the next paint flash or stone-built cairn. In extreme cases it may be necessary to take compass bearings and make progress from one to the other in this manner.

A third type of waymarking may also be encountered. This is the blue and white stripe of an *Alpine Route* that signifies a more challenging route which may involve glacier crossing or some scrambling.

Currently the most difficult paths are found on:

- Stage 3 on the descent from the Fenêtre d'Arpette to Champex
- Landslides in early 2018 on Stage 3 on the ascent to the Fenêtre d'Arpette have been well protected but could happen again
- Stage 6 between the Cabane du Mont Fort and the Col Termin where the spectacular Sentier des Chamois is exposed to rockfall
- The Col de la Chaux route, an alternative route on Stage 6
- Stage 6 between Col de Louvie and Col de Prafleuri where the route makes a traverse of a large area of rocks and boulders
- On the approach to, and crossing of, Col de Riedmatten (an option on Stage 7)
- Along the Europaweg on the final two stages leading to Zermatt. On this impressive and visually spectacular trail many exposed sections have been safeguarded with fixed rope handrails, and on several occasions the way crosses potentially hazardous areas where rockfall is a concern. Warning signs have been fixed that urge walkers to hurry across the danger areas.

SWISS ROUTE 6

Several stages of the Chamonix–Zermatt trail follow signs for Swiss National Walking Route 6 – The Alpine Passes Trail. This ultra long-distance trail runs from Chur in the Graubünden region to St-Gingolph on Lac Léman at the foot of the Dents du Midi. The whole route is 610km with 37,500m of ascent, and is reckoned to require 34 stages.

Stages of the Chamonix-Zermatt trail with Route 6 waymarking are:

- Stage 3 – the Bovine route to Champex

- Stage 6 – from Cabane de Louvie (joining the main route shortly after Col Termin) to Prafleuri

- Stage 7 – over the Pas de Chèvres to Arolla from Prafleuri

- Stage 8 – from Arolla to La Sage

- Stage 9A – the Col de Torrent route from La Sage to the Moiry Barrage

- Stage 10A – from the Moiry Barrage to Zinal over the Col de Sorebois

- Stage 11A/B – from Zinal via the Hôtel Weisshorn over the Meidpass to Gruben

- Stage 12 – from Gruben over the Augstbordpass to St Niklaus

Waymarking

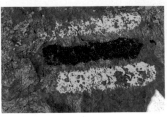

SAFETY IN THE MOUNTAINS

Although the route is mostly well signed (without ever mentioning the Chamonix to Zermatt Haute Route) with good paths for the majority of the way, and with working farms and villages at frequent intervals along the route, there are also wild and remote sections where an accident could have serious consequences. It should be recognised that participation in any mountain activity places a need for personal responsibility and self-reliance, for all mountain areas – the Alps as much as any – contain a variety of objective dangers for the unwary, and the long-distance walker should be prepared to deal with any hazards that arise.

Plan each day's walk carefully. Study the route outline, the amount of height to be gained and lost, and the time required to reach your destination. None of the stages described are particularly long, but in case you are tempted to double up, make sure you have enough hours of daylight in which to cross the day's pass and descend to the safety of the next valley, or to where a night's lodging may be had, before nightfall. Carry a few

emergency food rations and a first-aid kit. Know how to read a map and compass, and watch for signs of deteriorating weather. Never be too proud to turn back if it is safer to do so than to continue in the face of an oncoming storm or on a trail that has become unjustifiably dangerous.

In the unhappy event of an accident, stay calm. Move yourself and, if feasible, the injured person (with care not to aggravate the injury) away from any imminent danger of stonefall or avalanche, and apply immediate first aid. Keep the victim warm, using any spare clothes available. Make a careful written note of the precise location and assessment of the injury, and if you have a mobile phone (and can get a signal) call for assistance: tel 144, or tel 1414 which calls out helicopter rescue – this should only be used if absolutely essential. Alternatively, send for help while someone remains with the injured member.

The international distress call is a series of six signals (blasts on a whistle and – after dark – flashes with a torch) spaced evenly for a minute, followed by one minute's pause, then repeat with a further six signals. The reply is

The 500-metre Charles Kuonen Hängebrücke on the Europaweg on Stage 14

The Glacier de Cheilon from the top of the ladders at the Pas de Chèvres on Stage 7

three signals per minute followed by a minute's pause.

There is **no free mountain rescue service** in Switzerland and no free hospital treatment but EHIC cards for European (currently including UK) and Australian visitors are valid. The result of an emergency could therefore be extremely costly. Be adequately insured, and be cautious. The addresses of several specialist insurance companies dealing with mountain walking/trekking holidays are given in Appendix C.

Leave a copy of your travel itinerary and insurance details with a responsible friend or relative at home, and carry photocopies of important documents with you – information pages of your passport, insurance certificate, travel tickets, etc – as well as an emergency home contact address and telephone number.

WILDLIFE AND PLANTS

The Pennine Alps contain the richest flora in all Switzerland. One of the factors responsible for this is the mixture of limestone, gneiss and schistose rocks, which encourages calcipile (lime-loving) plants to flourish in some areas, and calcifuge varieties in others. Climatic considerations also play an important role, as does the marked difference in altitude between valley bed and the upper plant zone. Walkers who daily cross the high passes in a traverse of the region – particularly in the early summer – will wander through a number of successive plant zones, and it's not necessary to be a trained botanist to enjoy the variety of flowers and shrubs on show. There are, however, several handy well-illustrated guidebooks available that provide at-a-glance information on specific flowers such as *Alpine Flowers* by Gillian Price (Cicerone 2014).

There will be all the expected varieties, from gentian to edelweiss, from alpenrose to crimson-eyed primulas, and many more besides. This is not

Gentians surviving into the autumn

the place to list them all. Newcomers to the Alps may be surprised to find that it is not only the meadowlands that reward with bloom, but that even the high, seemingly lifeless cliff faces, screes and glacier-bordering moraines have their own species of flowering plants, and it is often such discoveries that make days in the mountains so memorable.

Of all creatures native to the Alps the one most likely to be seen on this walk is the engaging marmot (*Marmota marmota*). On many days you will no doubt first hear a sharp shrill whistle as you cross a boulder slope or wander a high alp on the borders of grassland and scree. This is the marmot's warning cry, and you may then see two or three brown furry creatures scurrying for cover.

The marmot is a gregarious animal, living in colonies among a variety of mountain and valley locations in burrows whose entrance holes may be seen from some of the footpaths on the walk. They grow to the size of a large hare and weigh up to 10kg (22lb), hibernating in winter for around five months, then emerging in spring when the snow cover melts. Their young are born during the early summer when you may be lucky enough to catch sight of kitten-sized creatures romping or playfully fighting in the short grass of the upper hillsides.

Chamois (*Rupicapra rupicapra*), or *Gemse* in German, are rarely seen at close quarters, but in the high mountain regions just below the snowline it is not unusual to spy a small herd picking its way with commendable ease over excessively steep terrain. On occasion they can be seen grazing on the forest fringe. From a distance it is possible to mistake chamois, with their small curving horns, for female or young ibex. Ibex, however, have a stockier body.

Ibex (*Capra ibex*) are also known as *bouquetin* (French) or *steinbock* (German). These squat, sturdy animals live and graze in herds – one noble buck with a harem of females. The male sports a pair of majestic, scimitar-shaped horns marked with a series of knobbles, like arthritic joints, that are used in battle as they fight for control over the herds, usually in the autumn rut.

On the scenic belvedere from Cabane du Mont Fort to Col Termin, known as the Sentier des Chamois

(Stage 6), ibex are likely to be seen at close quarters. A large herd lives nearby on a hillside designated as a wildlife sanctuary. Another herd may be seen near Cabane de Prafleuri.

MAPS

Maps of the Swiss survey, Landeskarte der Schweiz (LS/Carte Nationale de la Suisse, www.swisstopo.ch), are among the finest in the world. By artistic use of shading, contours and colouring, the line of ridges and rock faces, the flow of glaciers and streams, the curve of an amphitheatre, narrow cut of a glen, the expanse of a lake and forest cover of a hillside all announce themselves clearly. A picture of the country immediately leaps from the paper.

A list of the maps recommended for each stage of the route is given below. In each case I have chosen the 1:50,000 series as this should be perfectly adequate for most needs. The greater detail provided by the 1:25,000 series is not likely to be required on this route, given the amount of waymarking on the ground. (No fewer than nine sheets would be needed of 1:25,000 scale.) Addresses of map suppliers are given in Appendix C.

Standard coverage at 1:50,000 scale runs into five sheets (numbers 282T, 283T, 273T, 274T and 284T), each of which highlights major walking routes in red. Though not highlighting individual routes, the LS has also published two large sheets which cover the whole area crossed

Two hours from Gasenried, a viewpoint looks onto the Ried glacier (Stage 13)

41

by the Walker's Haute Route. These are:

- 5027T Grand St Bernard–Combins–Arolla
- 5028T Monte Rosa–Matterhorn.

It is important to source the latest version of the Landeskarte maps showing walking routes in red (and the alpine paths in blue). The versions without these overlays show the paths as dashed black lines that are hard to find and follow. Older versions may show paths that have been superseded, a much more common event in the Alps than elsewhere.

In addition, the Kümmerly + Frey 1:60,000 waterproof walking maps cover the route in three sheets:

- 22 Grand St Bernard–Dents du Midi (adequate for the stretch in France)
- 23 Val d'Anniviers/Val d'Hérens
- 24 Zermatt–Saas Fee. The Kümmerly + Frey maps also clearly show mountain walking routes.

The appropriate Swiss maps show the sections in France between Chamonix and the border at the Col de Balme.

Landeskarte der Schweiz 1:50,000 mapping	
LS 5027T Grand St Bernard–Combins–Arolla 1:50,000	Stages 1, 2, 3, 4, 5, 6, 7, 8
LS 282T Martigny 1:50,000	Stages 1, 2, 3, 4, 5
LS 283T Arolla 1:50,000	Stages 5, 6, 7, 8, 9, 10
LS 5028T Monte Rosa–Matterhorn 1:50,000	Stages 8, 9, 10, 11, 12, 13, 14, 13A/14A
LS 273T Montana 1:50,000	Stages 9, 10, 11
LS 274T Visp 1:50,000	Stages 11, 12, 13, 13A/14A
LS 284T Mischabel 1:50,000	Stages 13, 13A/14A
Kümmerly + Frey 1:60,000 mapping	
22 Grand St Bernard–Dents du Midi	Stages 1, 2, 3, 4, 5, 6
23 Val d'Anniviers–Val d'Hérens	Stages 6, 7, 8, 9, 10, 11
24 Zermatt–Saas Fee	Stages 9, 10, 11, 12, 13, 14, 13A/14A

The view at evening from Cabane Bella Tola (Stage 11A)

RECOMMENDED APPS

Several apps are helpful for travel and walking in the Swiss mountains.

MeteoSwiss An excellent weather app from the Swiss national weather agency. As you might expect it tends to perform a little better than more general weather apps, although it can take a little while to get the hang of.

Swiss Map An online mapping resource from the Swiss national mapping agency, giving access to maps of the country at all scales down to 1:25000. It is possible to buy annual subscriptions or buy and download specific tiles and areas for offline use. It includes a separate hiking trails layer showing all designated footpaths, including those on the Haute Route in Switzerland which is needed to get the full benefit of the app. (Other mapping apps also have Swiss mapping available, usually without the trails overlay.)

SBB Mobile Complete Swiss public transport including trains, buses, cablecars and anything else that moves. Ticket purchase in the app is straightforward. In 2018 tickets bought over a day before travel were significantly cheaper than those bought on the day.

USING THIS GUIDE

A brief word of explanation about this guidebook. Distances are given throughout in kilometres and metres. Heights quoted are in metric too. These details are taken from GPS and other measurements on the route. However, by using different devices, or different settings on the same device, you may find you get different results from your

The view back from Col de Torrent – both the Combin and Mont Blanc can still be seen (Stage 9A)

GPS system. Please do let Cicerone know (updates@cicerone.co.uk) if you get materially different measures.

Likewise, times are approximate only and make no allowance for rest stops or photographic interruptions – for these you will need to add another 25–50% to the day's total. Inevitably these times will be found slow by some walkers, fast by others. By comparing your times with those given here (or quoted on signposts along the route) you will soon discover how much our pace differs, and adjustments can then be made when calculating your own progress through the day.

Throughout the text route directions 'left' and 'right' apply to the direction of travel, whether in ascent, descent or traverse. However, when used in reference to the banks of glaciers or streams, 'left' and 'right' indicate the direction of flow, ie: looking downwards. Where doubts might occur, a compass direction is also given.

The following abbreviations have been used in the guide:
- ATM: cashpoints (automated teller machines)
- C–Z: Chamonix to Zermatt, the Walker's Haute Route
- hr: hours
- km: kilometres
- LS: Landeskarte der Schweiz (maps)
- m: metres
- min: minutes
- PTT: post office
- SAC: Swiss Alpine Club
- TMB: Tour of Mont Blanc

Facilities are indicated on the route maps and on elevation profiles, as shown in the key.

Finally, I have made every effort to check the route as described for accuracy, and it is to the best of my belief that the guidebook goes to press with all details correct. However, changes do occur from time to time with paths rerouted and certain landmarks altered. Check www.cicerone.co.uk/1048/updates for updates. Should you discover any changes that are necessary (or can recommend additions with regard to accommodation, places of refreshment, etc), a message to updates@cicerone.co.uk would be gratefully received.

INFORMATION AT A GLANCE

Currencies From Chamonix to Col de Balme (Stages 1–2) the euro is used; thereafter it's the Swiss franc (CHF) – 100 centimes (Fr)/rappen (Ger) = CHF1. But note that the euro is often acceptable in Trient and Champex, although change will be given in Swiss francs. Most credit cards are accepted in Swiss hotels, but cash will usually be needed in mountain huts, although this is steadily changing as improved online payment methods become available. Carry plenty of ready cash with you as there are few ATMs and even fewer banks along the route.

Formalities Visas are not currently required in France or Switzerland for holders of a valid UK passport or other EU nationals. Visitors from other countries should enquire at their local French and Swiss embassies.

Health precautions At the time of writing no vaccinations are required by visitors entering France or Switzerland unless they've been in an infected area within 14 days of arrival. Although there are no endemic contagious diseases here, the Ixodes tick, whose bite can cause tick-borne encephilitis (TBE), exists in several alpine regions, as in much of Central Europe. Risk is seasonal, from March to September, so summer trekkers may be vulnerable. An injection of TBE immunoglobulin gives short-term protection; ask your GP for advice. Any medical treatment in Switzerland must be paid for, although the European Health Insurance Card (EHIC) is currently valid in both France and Switzerland – but note its limitations. It is no substitute for health insurance, so make sure you have adequate cover that includes personal accident, sickness and rescue. (See Appendix C for a list of specialist insurers.)

International dialling codes When phoning to France from the UK, use 0033 (011 33 from the USA); for Switzerland use 0041 (011 41 from the USA). To phone the UK from France or Switzerland, the code is 0044. In all cases remember to delete the initial 0 of the area code after dialling the international code. Where phone booths exist (which is rare) they are cashless, operated by phonecard. Telephone cards (*télécarte* in France, *taxcard* in Switzerland) may be bought in post offices, tobacconists, newsagents and some railway stations.

Languages spoken French is the main language spoken throughout the Walker's Haute Route until you reach the Turtmanntal on Stage 11A/Stage 11B; thereafter it is German – or rather, *Schwyzerdütsch*. English is understood in many of the hotels, dortoirs and refuges along the way, but an effort to communicate in French (to Zinal) or German (after Zinal) would be appreciated.

Weather on the web www.meteofrance.com provides three-day forecasts. For the Swiss Alps try www.meteoschweiz.ch/web/en.html which gives daily and five-day forecasts.

CHAMONIX TO ZERMATT

Looking south over the Lac de Moiry towards the Dent Blanche (Stages 9A and 10A)

STAGE 1
Chamonix – Argentière

Start	Chamonix (1037m)
Distance	9km
Total ascent	300m
Total descent	85m
Time	2hr 15min
High point	Argentière (1251m)
Accommodation	Chamonix: hotels, youth hostel, camping; Les Praz de Chamonix (35min): hotels, camping; Argentière: hotels, gîte
Transport options	Train and bus (Chamonix–Argentière)

This initial, very short stage is suggested as a prelude for walkers who arrive in Chamonix late in the day and wish to get a few kilometres under their boots before seeking overnight accommodation. Those who arrive early and fresh enough from their travels can, of course, combine this with Stage 2 and continue over Col de Balme to Trient for a 7–8hr day.

It's a valley walk without any passes to tackle. But it's a pleasant walk all the same, with a few short ascents to contend with. It begins by threading a way among the crowds that throng the streets of Chamonix and heads upvalley on the road leading out of town, but then takes a path through woods and across open glades with a wonderful introductory view of the Drus standing guard over the Mer de Glace. Crossing the Arveyron the walk enters Les Praz de Chamonix, then over the river Arve onto another woodland path that is followed most of the way to Argentière.

Chamonix's valley is dominated by the Mont Blanc massif whose jagged aiguilles form fenceposts of granite and whose glaciers hang in sheets of arctic splendour above the town and its neighbouring forests. On the walk to Argentière there are several opportunities to gaze upon such scenes, while the bare northern wall with the russet-coloured Aiguilles Rouges is largely hidden from view.

As early as 1741 Chamonix – then a small village – was 'discovered' by Richard Pococke and William Windham, whose *Account of the Glaciers or Ice Alps in Savoy* sowed the seeds of popularity for the valley; a popularity that has steadily increased from a lowly trickle to the present-day deluge of tourists who threaten an overkill, with around a million visitors per year in Chamonix alone.

Footpaths along the valley are busy during the summer and will remain so for the first three stages; that is, until the route of the Tour of Mont Blanc (TMB) has been left behind after Champex. During the high season there's likely to be a heavy demand for accommodation. Booking in advance is recommended.

From Chamonix **railway station** walk down the main street, Avenue Michel Croz, alongside shops and restaurants, and take the first road breaking to the right. This is Rue Whymper, which leads to a roundabout opposite the École Nationale de Ski et d'Alpinisme. Continue straight ahead along the road signed to Les Praz and Argentière, soon leaving the town behind.

Shortly after passing the Chamonix–Mont Blanc road sign (15min from the station) note a bus stop on the left,

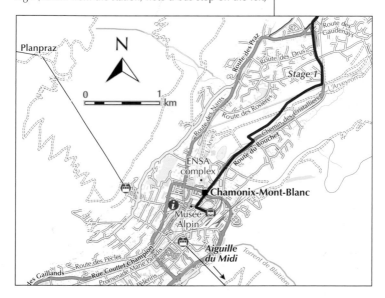

CHAMONIX (1037M)

The busy centre of Chamonix, which will soon be left behind for much quieter walking

With the close proximity of Mont Blanc, Chamonix has always been at the forefront of alpine mountaineering, and during the development of alpinism in the 19th century it became a serious rival to Zermatt. Today it is unquestionably the leading mountaineering centre of Europe, if not the world. But the town's importance extends beyond the limits of mountaineering, for in winter it is a major ski resort, while in summer it attracts a deluge of general tourists. Chamonix has plenty to occupy them, including the cablecar to the summit of the Aiguille du Midi, and from there the possibility of traversing the whole range by cableway to Entrèves, near Courmayeur in Italy. The railway to Montenvers has long been one of the most popular excursions, with its climax being superb views along the Mer de Glace to the Grandes Jorasses.

The Chamonix valley, of course, offers excellent walking opportunities. In particular it is a base for the Tour of Mont Blanc trek. The summer season has been extended by the highly successful Ultra Trail du Mont Blanc (UTMB) race, which uses, in the main, the Tour of Mont Blanc trail and takes place just before the end of August. If your walking coincides with the UTMB the race is an inspiring sight. See *Mont Blanc Walks* by Hilary Sharp (Cicerone Press), *Chamonix Mountain Adventures*, also by Hilary Sharp, and *Chamonix Trail Running* by Kingsley Jones. Although the classic Tour of Mont Blanc does not actually visit Chamonix itself, it does traverse the valley. See *Tour of Mont Blanc* by Kev Reynolds (Cicerone Press).

Hotels, youth hostel, camping, restaurants, shops, banks, PTT, tourist information, railway, buses, cableways and funicular, **www.chamonix.com**.

and a sign on the right to La Frasse and Les Coverays. Immediately after the bus stop turn left over a bridge, then take the right-hand of two paths. This leads through the Bois du Bouchet. On coming to a crossing track turn right and soon gain a very fine view of the spear-like Drus ahead. At a crossing road continue ahead, and when the path veers right to enter a tunnel, leave it in favour of a minor path which takes you onto the main road where it crosses the **Arveyron** (30min). Turn left and walk into **Les Praz de Chamonix** (1062m, 40min, hotels, camping, restaurants).

When you reach a roundabout cross directly ahead beside a small church in the direction of Argentière and Martigny. Immediately after passing the Chalet Hotel Le Castel the road curves to the right where you gain another splendid view of the Drus. Take the first turning left and wander past the Hôtel Le Labrador and its **golf course**. Through a golf club car park continue ahead on a gravel track which soon crosses the **river Arve**. Ignore the initial path on the right, but stay on the track which curves right just beyond. The track becomes a narrow metalled lane. When it forks continue ahead and shortly come to the café/bar **Le Paradis des Praz** (refreshments). Beyond this the way continues as a pleasant forest walk beside a stream.

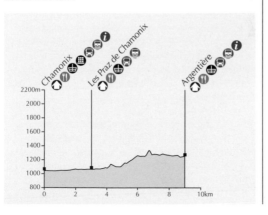

Ignore all bridges across to the right-hand side of the Arve, and at path junctions follow signs for Argentière. About 1hr 5min from the start the way forks near the Pont de la Corva (1092m). Do not cross the bridge but stay on the left of the river and climb the wooded slope on the Petit Balcon Sud (the name of this low-level trail from Chamonix to Argentière). From here to Argentière there are several junctions, all well signed. Remain on the Petit Balcon Sud; in woods most of the way it's an undulating trail which climbs over 200m to its maximum altitude, then slopes downhill only to climb again. There are several bench seats, but few open views.

THE GOLDEN AGE OF MOUNTAINEERING

The Haute Route begins by wandering down Chamonix's main street, Avenue Michel Croz, named after one of the finest guides of the Golden Age of Mountaineering, a man whose talent and skills were discovered by Alfred Wills and then put to good use by Edward Whymper. Croz was a Chamonix guide (born in Le Tour in 1830) whose list of first ascents includes the Barre des Écrins, Mont Dolent, Aiguille d'Argentière, Dent Blanche, Grandes Jorasses and the crossing of the Moming Pass above Zinal. In 1865 Croz was in Whymper's party that made the first ascent of the Matterhorn, but tragically was killed on the descent. (See *Scrambles Amongst the Alps* by Edward Whymper.)

On leaving Avenue Michel Croz the route turns into Rue Whymper. Edward Whymper will forever be remembered as the man who first climbed the Matterhorn, and as such is known far beyond the somewhat limited circle of active mountaineers. Whymper was a London-born wood engraver who first visited the Alps in 1860 in order to make a series of sketches for the publisher William Longman. The following year he began a remarkable climbing career (often with Michel Croz) that included first ascents of the Barre des Écrins, the aiguilles of Trélatête and Argentière, Grand Cornier, Grandes Jorasses (west summit), Aiguille Verte and, of course, the Matterhorn.

He did little climbing in the Alps after the Matterhorn tragedy, but explored farther afield – making journeys to Greenland, the Andes of South America and three trips to the Canadian Rockies. His *Scrambles Amongst the Alps* is still considered to be one of the finest of all mountaineering books, and is frequently reprinted. Whymper died in Chamonix at the age of 71.

The path takes you down almost to the level of the railway, follows it for a short distance then climbs briefly before sloping downhill again, coming onto a track by some houses. Walk ahead along the track to arrive in the main street in **Argentière**.

The Aiguille du Dru, seen from Les Praz de Chamonix on the way to Argentière

ARGENTIÈRE (1251M)

Argentière is a compact village at the upper end of the Chamonix valley. The original village stands on the true left bank of the Arve below the terminal moraine of the Argentière Glacier, and is an attractive huddle of chalets and a small church. Argentière makes a low-key alternative to Chamonix for a mountaineering or skiing base. The 'new' village which has grown astride the main valley road has a range of accommodation, plenty of restaurants, food stores and a tourist information office.

Accommodation at Gîte d'étape Le Belvedere, 52 dortoir places, meals provided (tel 04 50 18 50 66, **www.gitelebelvedere.com**); lower-priced hotel: Hôtel Les Randonneurs (tel 04 50 54 02 80, **www.lesrandonneurs.fr**). Restaurants, shops, PTT, tourist information (tel 04 50 53 99 98, **www.argentiere-mont-blanc.com**), railway and bus links with Chamonix.

If you have difficulty finding accommodation in Argentière, try Gîte d'étape Le Moulin in Les Frasserands about 2km upvalley, 38 places, open all year (tel 04 50 54 05 37 and 06 82 33 34 54).

STAGE 2
Argentière – Col de Balme – Trient

Start	Argentière (1251m)
Distance	15km; 18.5km via Les Grands
Total ascent	1000m; 1200m via Les Grands
Total descent	975m
Time	5hr 30 min; 7hr 30 min via Les Grands
High point	Col de Balme (2204m)
Accommodation	Le Tour (1hr 20min): hotel, gîte; Col de Balme (3hr 30min): refuge; Le Peuty (5hr 15min): gîte, camping; Trient: dortoirs
Transport options	Bus (Argentière–Le Tour); gondola and chairlift (Le Tour-Charamillon-Les Grandes Otanes near Col de Balme)
Alternative routes	Col de Balme to Trient via L'Arolette or via Refuge Les Grands and the Trient valley *bisse*.

For a first full day's walking this is a convenient and relatively undemanding stage. There's plenty of height to gain and lose, but the crossing of Col de Balme is not at all severe and walkers have an opportunity to get into their stride with ease. On the way to the pass, views looking back through the length of the Chamonix valley are dominated by Mont Blanc and its aiguilles, while the col itself gives a magnificent view of the Monarch of the Alps shining its great snow dome and sending long tentacles into the valley.

The Swiss frontier runs through Col de Balme, so all the descent (and the rest of the walk to Zermatt) will be within Swiss territory. Vistas of Mont Blanc are shunted into memory, although in days to come sudden surprise views will draw the eye back to the west and that great crown of snow.

The valley of Trient into which you descend is green and pastoral. There are no major peaks nearby, of either snow or rock, to match the grandeur of France behind you, but the scene from the col is not short of beauty, for to the north a line of mountains indicates the crest of the Bernese Alps, with Les Diablerets, Wildhorn and Wildstrubel just discernible.

The two alternative descents from the Col de Balme to Trient provide very different routes and views. The first, via L'Arolette, is slightly longer but

scenically more interesting than the standard direct route. The second, via
Refuge Les Grands, uses a quieter variant of the TMB but this option would
be too long for a first day if you started from Chamonix.

From the centre of Argentière take the road to the right
(east), to pass the village post office and Office du
Tourisme, and cross the river (**l'Arve**) with the Glacier
d'Argentière seen directly ahead.

> The **Glacier d'Argentière** flows from the great basin
> formed by the curving ridges of the Tour Noir, Mont
> Dolent, Aiguille de Triolet, Les Courtes and Les
> Droites. Mont Dolent is the lynchpin of this system,
> and on its summit the frontiers of France, Italy and
> Switzerland meet.

At a junction of streets bear right into the Chemin de
la Moraine, and you will come to the line of the Mont
Blanc Express **railway**. Pass beneath this and onto a track
going ahead towards woods where you join the Petit
Balcon Nord. Shortly after passing a chalet on the right,
you'll see another set back on the left. On coming to a
second chalet on the left, take the path beside it which

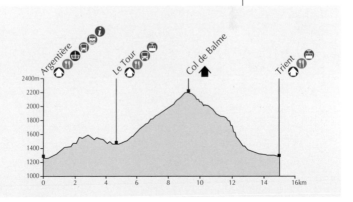

57

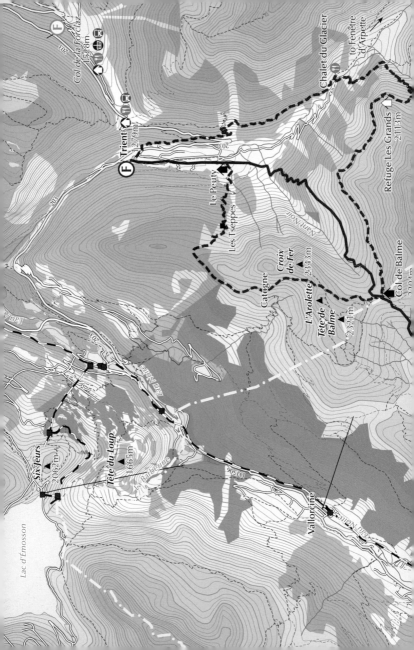

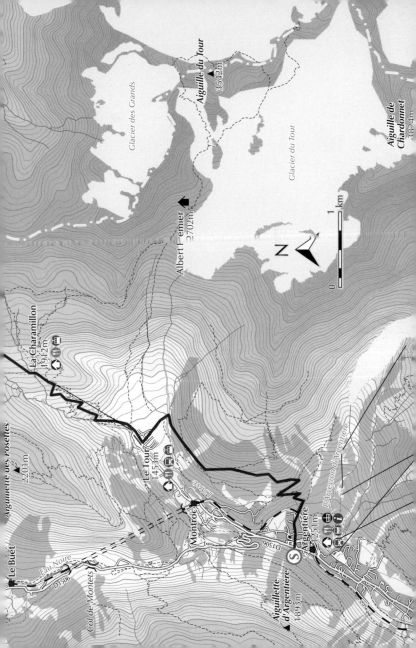

The village of Le Tour from the trail

joins the main Petit Balcon Nord at a signed junction. Turn left towards Le Tour.

Rising steadily among trees you will come to a path junction (20min) where you continue straight ahead. In another 20min there is a second junction where again you keep ahead. Emerging from the woods the path narrows and gradually loses height with **Le Tour** seen below. Cross a stream draining the Glacier du Tour and walk on into the village (1hr 20 min).

> **LE TOUR (1453m)** Accommodation: Chalet Alpin du Tour (CAF gîte) 87 places, open April to end of September (tel 04 50 54 04 16, **www.chaletdutour. ffcam.fr**); Hôtel l'Olympique (tel 04 50 54 01 04, **www.hotel-olympique-chamonix.com**). Restaurant, water supply, public toilets, telephone, bus to Chamonix, gondola lift to Charamillon.

If you prefer to take the easy way to Col de Balme, ride the gondola lift to Charamillon, then take the chairlift to Les Grandes Otanes, from which a short contouring path leads to the col.

Walk to the roadhead by the Télécabine Le Tour Col de Balme. ◄

The main path to Col de Balme passes along the right-hand side of the gondola lift station and continues ahead on a broad track/ski piste. About 10min from the gondola station a signed path strikes ahead to the right and twists up to the middle station of the gondola lift, **Chalet de Charamillon** (1912m, 2hr 30min, refreshments).

Above Charamillon a path branches to the right away from the main track on the way to the popular Albert Premier refuge, first passing the **Gîte d'Alpage** (20 places, open mid-June to mid-September, tel 04 50 54 17 07, refreshments). Ignore this option and maintain direction to continue up the track, but a short while later take the footpath which splits off to the right and rises above the track. The gradient soon eases and the path gains height without undue effort to reach the **Chalet-Refuge Col de Balme** (3hr 30min).

> **CHALET-REFUGE COL DE BALME (2204m)** The refuge has 20 places, open end of June to mid-September (tel +33 60 70 61 630). It stands on the unmarked Franco/Swiss border and purchases can be made in either Euros or Swiss francs.

Standing astride the Franco/Swiss border on the Col de Balme with a magnificent view of the Mont Blanc range ('If that view does not thrill you you are better away from the Alps,' wrote RLG Irving),

Refuge Col de Balme on the Franco-Swiss border, after a summer snowstorm

The Chamonix valley and Mont Blanc seen from the trail to the Col de Balme

the **Chalet-Refuge Col de Balme** – or rather each of its predecessors in turn – was for centuries a bone of contention between the men of Chamonix and those of Swiss Valais, and was burnt down and rebuilt several times. It's interesting to note that the col is measured at 2191m by the French, and 2204m by the Swiss. As the refuge is entered from the Swiss side, it's reckoned to be in Swiss territory, although its telephone number is French.

Groups of ebullient walkers occupied all the seats outside the refuge, and most of those inside too. To a man (and a woman) they were all tackling the TMB and enjoying the cameraderie such a sociable walk inspires, greeting each new arrival with rude remarks, having established an easy rapport during the days in which they'd shared the same paths, valleys and passes. They were heading south on the closing stages of their classic walk, while we were going in the opposite direction, against the tide, as it were. I looked back at Mont Blanc, then ahead to a grid of distant ridges that both teased and enticed. Col de Balme held the key to a wonderland.

MONT BLANC

As the highest mountain in Western Europe Mont Blanc (4807m) has been the focus of mountaineering attention for more than two centuries. In 1760 wealthy Genevese scientist Horace-Bénédict de Saussure (1740–99) offered a prize for the first man to reach its summit. Several attempts were made in the ensuing years, but it was not until 8 August 1786 that Michel-Gabriel Páccard, the Chamonix doctor, and Jacques Balmat, a crystal hunter, reached the top. (Saussure himself made the third ascent in 1787.) Tourist ascents followed, then attention was focused on neighbouring aiguilles and new routes to already claimed summits.

Among the outstanding developments mention should be made of the Brenva Ridge in 1865, Peuterey Ridge (1927), Route Major (1928), Gervasutti Pillar (1951) and Central Pillar of Freney in 1961. But while practically every face, pillar, ridge and couloir has been explored, Mont Blanc still retains its charisma, and to non-mountaineers no less, its undisputed grace and beauty. For a history of the mountain, see *Savage Snows* by Walt Unsworth (Hodder & Stoughton, 1986).

The col makes a wonderful viewpoint. To the south stands the snowy mass of Mont Blanc and its guardian aiguilles – Aiguille Verte and the Drus being predominant in that view, while the Aiguilles Rouges line the right-hand wall of the valley.

There are three ways in which to continue from Col de Balme:

- the **direct route (1hr 30min)** to Trient via Le Peuty described as the main Stage 2;
- a slightly **longer option (2hr)** by way of L'Arolette, Catogne and Les Tseppes – described at the end of this stage;
- **a longer option (3hr 30min)** via Refuge Les Grands; also described at the end of this stage.

With your back to the refuge and Mont Blanc, go left on the footpath for 20 metres to a signpost at a footpath junction, then branch right to begin the descent. The path goes down in long loops at first (water supply at the hut of Les Herbagères), but once you enter forest the way steepens with tighter zig-zags. It brings you into a rough pastureland where you bear left to cross the **Nant Noir** stream and walk down to **Le Peuty** (5hr 15min).

> **LE PEUTY (1328m)** Self-catering (meals available in Trient) gîte accommodation and camping at Refuge du Peuty, 20 places, open mid-June to mid-September (tel 027 722 09 38 or 078 719 29 83, **www. happytracks.net**).

Continue down the road for a further 15min to the village of **Trient** (5hr 30min).

TRIENT (1279M)

A small village set in a narrowing of the valley of the same name below La Forclaz. In spite of its being the first Swiss community met on this walk, it is nevertheless very French in both architecture and atmosphere. Its location is ideal for tackling the crossing of either the Fenêtre d'Arpette or Col de la Forclaz and the Bovine route for the next stage to Champex.

Rooms and dortoir accommodation at Auberge Mont Blanc, 70 places, open all year (tel 027 767 15 05, **www.aubergemontblanc.com**); and La Grande Ourse, 38 dortoir places, 18 beds, open all year (tel 027 722 17 54, **www.la-grande-ourse.ch**); PTT, Postbus link with Martigny. Tourist information: **www.trient.ch**.

If you have difficulty finding accommodation here, try Hôtel du Col de la Forclaz 3km uphill to the east; 40 places in bedrooms and dortoir (tel 027 722 26 88, **www.coldelaforclaz.ch**).

Alternative descent from Col de Balme to Trient via L'Arolette

This descent to Trient from Col de Balme is slightly longer, a little more demanding, but more scenically interesting than the standard direct route described above.

Arriving at Col de Balme walk past the refuge and 1min later, where the path forks and the direct route to Trient branches right, continue ahead. The path curves round the hillside and forks again. Take the right branch, which rises gently and, 20min from the refuge, brings you onto the 2264m saddle of **L'Arolette** to gain a view ahead of the distant Emosson dam backed by Mont Ruan.

The path now descends the north side of the pass, sweeping down and across the steep grass flank of the **Croix de Fer**. On coming to a signed junction at 2110m above the alp buildings of **Catogne**, fork right on a path which contours across pastures and into larchwoods with a view across the Trient gorge. The way turns a spur into the Trient valley, from where you look through the length of the upper valley to the Aiguille du Tour flanked by the Glacier du Trient and the Glacier des Grands.

The descent into the valley takes you briefly into forest, then you gain another, but even better, view of the same mountain and its glaciers. About 5min later pass the two timber chalets of **Les Tseppes** (1932m), and shortly after re-enter forest for a steep, knee-crunching descent. At another junction within the forest (1750m) bear right (left is a longer option and is occasionally closed), and continue to descend in short steep zig-zags. When you reach a gravel track turn right downhill. The track soon loops back and the path down to **La Peuty** continues through pastures on the right. At La Peuty turn left down the road for 15min to reach **Trient** (2hr from Col de Balme). For accommodation in the village bear left. For Col de la Forclaz take the upper road.

Alternative descent from Col de Balme to Trient via Refuge Les Grands

This longer descent uses a quieter variant of the TMB, finishing either at Trient or the Col de la Forclaz. It passes Refuge Les Grands self-catering refuge which does not always have a guardian in residence, so if you plan to stay there it would be wise to carry food. Finishing at Forclaz gives a head start on the Bovine variant on Stage 3.

Using Refuge Les Grands could also allow the trekker to bypass Trient, a particularly busy spot with TMB walkers. The following day, after descending to the valley at Chalet du Glacier (Les Glaciers), climb directly to the Fenêtre d'Arpette to give a stage of similar length, time and ascent to the main Stage 3 from Trient. This, however, would add 600m more descent on top of the 1200m already required.

A few paces before reaching the Chalet-Refuge Col de Balme bear slightly right at a footpath junction signed to Les Grands, Chalet du Glacier and Col de la Forclaz. The path contours for about 5min, then descends a little along the right-hand hillside; in places the trail is narrow, but clear throughout. Having descended a short way it resumes a hillside traverse with views down to Trient and Col de la Forclaz.

About 45min from Col de Balme, and having crossed a rocky section, the path turns a spur to gain a view into the upper reaches of the Trient valley and across to the Fenêtre d'Arpette. Now the hillside is clothed with bilberry and alpenrose, and as the way advances so the path climbs again, with the Glacier du Trient seen ahead, and the smaller Glacier des Grands above to the right

The Glacier du Trient seen from the path from Refuge Les Grands

– superb alpine scenery. Topping a high point at about 2150m the **Refuge Les Grands** can be seen below. The path descends directly to it (5hr).

> **REFUGE LES GRANDS (2113m)** 15 places, cooking facilities, water supply; guardian sometimes in residence, open mid-June to mid-October; reservations (tel 026 662 13 33 or 07956 71934).

The path descends directly below the hut, quite steeply in places, and soon slants across a rock face with fixed cable for safety. It then resumes in steep zig-zags, passes a couple of small ruins and enters pinewoods. On coming to a fork in the path ignore the right hand option (which leads to Alpage des Petoudes) and continue ahead, eventually reaching another path junction by a footbridge spanning a glacial torrent.

Cross the bridge to another path junction. A few paces to the right **Chalet du Glacier** (1583m, 6hr) offers refreshments. The path which continues beyond it leads to the Fenêtre d'Arpette. Instead turn left alongside the Bisse du Trient (irrigation channel), then left again to descend through woods to **Trient** in 1hr.

Alternatively continue along the *bisse* on a charming near-level path to reach the Col de la Forclaz in another 50min from the Chalet du Glacier. For facilities at the Col de la Forclaz, see Stage 3A.

OPTIONS FROM TRIENT

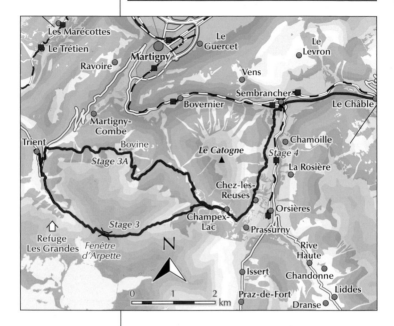

There are two contrasting routes from Trient through to Champex. The harder, higher route is via the Fenêtre d'Arpette, a mountain route over a well-known and popular trail with views over the Trient Glacier and the northern part of the Mont Blanc range. The Fenêtre itself is a tiny 'nick' in the ridge. The descent on its eastern side is both steep and loose.

The alternative is over the Bovine, a route of similar length but overlooking the Rhône valley with the opportunity for refreshments along the way. If you have started the trek slowly, or if the weather is poor and there is snow over the higher cols, then the Bovine is preferable. Although it is reckoned to be easier, it is still a fine walk and is in no way a second-best.

STAGE 3

Trient – Fenêtre d'Arpette – Champex

Start	Trient (1279m)
Distance	16km
Total ascent	1390m
Total descent	1200m
Time	7hr
High point	Fenêtre d'Arpette (2665m)
Accommodation	Arpette (6hr 15min): hotel/dortoir, camping; Champex: hotels, pensions, dortoirs, camping
Transport options	Postbus (Trient–Col de la Forclaz–Martigny); train (Martigny–Orsières); bus (Orsières–Champex)

The crossing of Fenêtre d'Arpette is a classic outing and one of the most demanding of the whole walk, particularly as it is met on the second or third day of the trek. The approach to it is full of interest, with the frozen cascades of the Glacier du Trient's icefall coming into view as you climb, while the descent into the lovely pastoral Val d'Arpette begins with a wilderness of scree and boulders, but finishes with joyful streams, spacious woods and meadows. These contrasts are bound to bring pleasure to all Haute Route trekkers, for it is in such contrasts that long-distance mountain routes gain much of their appeal.

The path is a good one practically all the way, but care should be exercised on the initial descent from the pass where scree then boulder fields are crossed. A twisted ankle here could have serious consequences.

At the end of the day Champex is the first 'real' Swiss village of the route, with attractive chalets facing the sun and boxes of flowers at the windows. It's a popular, welcoming little resort that has grown along the shores of a small reedy lake, and is noted for its magnificent alpine garden – considered by many to be the finest in Switzerland.

Above the church in Trient walk up the main Col de la Forclaz road to a sign by a stone cross on the left which directs the way to the Sentier du Bisse-Glacier along a

Looking up to the Glacier du Trient

Walkers who spent the night at the Hôtel du Col de la Forclaz (see Stage 3A) and plan to use the Fenêtre d'Arpette route should cross the road in front of the hotel where a signpost directs the path as Bisse du Trient – 1hr to the Chalet du Glacier.

broad grass track rising in long easy loops. At a junction of tracks continue ahead to regain the road (35min). Cross directly ahead onto the continuing track which soon narrows to a footpath, zig-zags again and comes to a lovely path along a *bisse* (irrigation watercourse) where you turn right. Follow this path all the way to the **Chalet du Glacier** (1583m, 1hr 15min, refreshments). ◄

The path forks at the Chalet du Glacier. Bear left and climb uphill to another fork. Once more take the left branch (the right-hand, lower, path goes to the glacier), where the climb to the pass begins in earnest, first among woods, then above these on a more open stretch with clear uninterrupted views onto the fast-receding glacier. As you gain height so the Aiguilles Dorées and Pointe d'Orny grow above you to the south.

At 1900m, there has been a substantial landslide and the path has been rerouted on wooden steps and is protected by a rope rail.

The gradient steepens, but the path is always clearly defined, even when crossing rocky slopes. Few paths allow such detailed study of an icefield in all its tortured

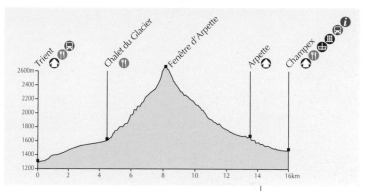

glory as this does, and views are consistently magnificent. The glacier is now sadly diminished from its former glory. But the pass remains a well-kept secret until you're almost there. A last scramble over a jumble of rocks brings you finally to the **Fenêtre d'Arpette** (2665m, 3hr 50min).

THE FENÊTRE D'ARPETTE

This wild and rocky cleft makes a splendid pass, for the ridge it breaches is very much a division; to the west all mountains and glaciers owe allegiance to Mont Blanc, while to the east lies a new world – a stony world rather than an arctic one, and it will be three more days before you again feel the brush of glacial air on your face. The three-day intermission goes from bare rocks to pasture and forest through a neat and tended landscape, a brief respite before the high mountains are regained. The Fenêtre d'Arpette is a geological hyphen, and from it you gaze eagerly to the east and south-east, where an array of ridges jostle the horizon and the Combin massif gleams a splash of white against the sky – a promise of good things to come.

The classic, scenically spectacular Tour of Mont Blanc makes a circuit of the Mont Blanc massif by way of the seven valleys that surround it. The TMB has numerous *variantes*, and one of them crosses the Fenêtre, so you are unlikely to be alone. The standard route is some 190km long and takes 10–12 days to complete. With some justification it is one of the most popular long-distance routes in Europe. See *Tour of Mont Blanc* by Kev Reynolds (Cicerone Press).

Trekkers taking it all in on the Fenêtre d'Arpette

We reached the pass in time to eat our lunch, emerging from a cool wind to bright sunshine and sun-warmed rocks on the Arpette side. But the walking world had come to the Fenêtre too, for everywhere we looked tanned bodies were spread across the rocks like basking seals. Not for nothing is this pass known locally as the Champs-Elysées. Thank the popularity of the Tour of Mont Blanc for that, for the pass is on a much-loved TMB Variante. More than 10,000 people a year walk that circuit. How was I to know they would all be gathered that very day on the Fenêtre d'Arpette?

At first the descent drops into a rough, stony bowl at the head of **Val d'Arpette**. Caution is advised for the initial 100m or so of vertical ascent, where each one of an assortment of paths is particularly steep and loose underfoot. Below this you cross a chaotic boulder field, descending a further 100m, before the path (waymarked over the boulders) treats you with more respect and eases (around 1hr from the col) into Val d'Arpette proper.

Pastures and fruiting shrubs are a welcome relief after the barren rocks of the upper valley, and in 2hr 15min from the pass you come to a group of farms where a track leads onto the right bank of the stream. Five minutes later you reach the **Relais d'Arpette** (6hr 10min).

RELAIS D'ARPETTE (1627m) 90 places in beds and dortoir, camping, refreshments, open from June to end-September (tel 027 783 12 21, **www. arpette.ch**).

Just beyond the hotel turn off the main track/road and take a footpath on the left that descends among trees and follows a stream. On coming to a bridge cross over, then go right on a footpath waymarked with yellow diamonds and occasional green stripes. Recross the stream and soon after bear left when the path forks.

The fast-running brook you now accompany is a leat, or *bisse* – a watercourse created to direct part of a stream into a new valley, or to bring water to otherwise dry farmland. The Valais region has many such watercourses. One was followed at the start of the day, and there will be

The U-shaped Arpette valley and the descent towards Champex

several more to follow in the days ahead. The path eventually brings you out of the woods at a small pond by a chairlift station. Go onto the road and bear right into **Champex** (7hr).

CHAMPEX (1466M)

Also known as Champex-Lac to emphasise its lakeside position, this modest-sized village has developed as an all-year resort. During the summer there's swimming in a heated pool, boating and fishing in the lake. The alpine garden (Jardin Alpin Flore-alpe) above the village on the hillside to the north contains more than 4000 plants, and is generally reckoned to be the finest collection in Switzerland.

Accommodation (hotels, pensions, dortoirs, camping), restaurants, shops, PTT, bus link with Orsières and Martigny. Tourist information: **www.champex.info**. Lower-priced accommodation: Ptarmigan (B&B), 6 places, open all year (tel 027 783 16 40); Pension En Plein Air, 61 places in dortoirs/beds, suitable for budget group accommodation, open mid-January to the end of September (tel 027 783 23 50, **www.pensionenpleinair.ch**). The long-standing Au Club Alpin was being completely renovated during 2018, and its future as accommodation is in doubt so check the website (**www.auclubalpin.ch**).

Arriving in Champex late in the afternoon we sought dortoir accommodation and were soon booked in at the Plein Air, to find comfortable beds in a dormitory with curtains dividing the room to allow a degree of privacy not normally experienced in such places. I went for a shower and came out at the same time as a Dutchman whom we'd met the previous evening in Trient. We both had wet towels and socks to dry so went onto the balcony outside our room to hang them out overnight. As we stood there, suddenly the balcony floor gave way beneath us and crashed onto the pavement, leaving the Dutchman and me hanging from the rail high above the street. We were wondering how to swing back into our room in safety when a shout from below caught our attention. It was a German trekker who'd also been in Trient the previous night. 'This looks good,' he called, waving his camera. 'Hold it there, I would like a photo of this.'

STAGE 3A

Trient – Col de la Forclaz – Alp Bovine – Champex

Start	Trient (1279m)
Distance	16km
Total ascent	1040m
Total descent	850m
Time	5hr 45min
High point	Above Alp Bovine (2049m)
Accommodation	Col de la Forclaz (45min): hotel, dortoir, camping; Alp Bovine (2hr 30min): emergency dortoir only; Champex d'en Haut (4hr 30min): auberge/gîte, hotel, Champex. hotels, pensions, dortoirs, camping
Transport options	Postbus (Trient–Col de la Forclaz–Martigny); train (Martigny–Orsières); bus (Orsières–Champex)

This route is the bad-weather alternative to the more demanding Fenêtre d'Arpette crossing, but it should not be assumed that it is an uninteresting walk, or indeed easy. Far from it. It's a green and pleasant way, among forest and pasture and with good views down into the Rhône valley and across to the Bernese Alps that rise on the northern side. Since this is the path of the main TMB (the Fenêtre route is a *variante*) it is well used, but the vast majority of walkers will be coming towards you.

From the church in Trient walk up to the main Col de la Forclaz road and bear right along it. Look for a sign on the left to Sentier du Bisse-Glacier by a stone cross. A broad grass track swings up the hillside in easy loops, and at junctions you follow signs for Col de la Forclaz (soon leaving the *bisse* route), and eventually the track brings you onto the road. Cross the road over the footbridge, and climb steeply at first through woods, to finally emerge at **Col de la Forclaz** (50min).

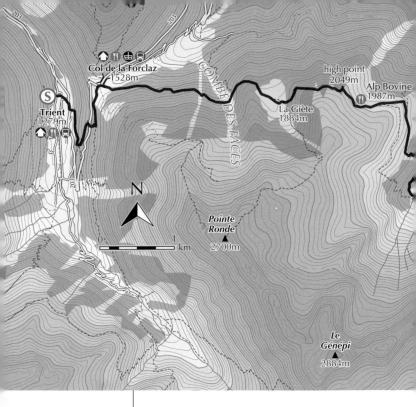

COL DE LA FORCLAZ (1528m) Accommodation at Hôtel du Col de la Forclaz; 65 places in rooms and dortoirs (tel 027 722 26 88, **www.coldelaforclaz. ch**), camping, refreshments, shop.

COL DE LA FORCLAZ

The path from Chalet du Glacier to the col was originally laid with rails in order to transport ice from the Trient glacier to the hotel on the pass. The road which crosses Col de la Forclaz, thereby linking Martigny with Chamonix was built between 1825 and 1887. The first motor vehicles crossed in 1912, with a maximum approved speed of 18km per hour – none were allowed to make the journey by night.

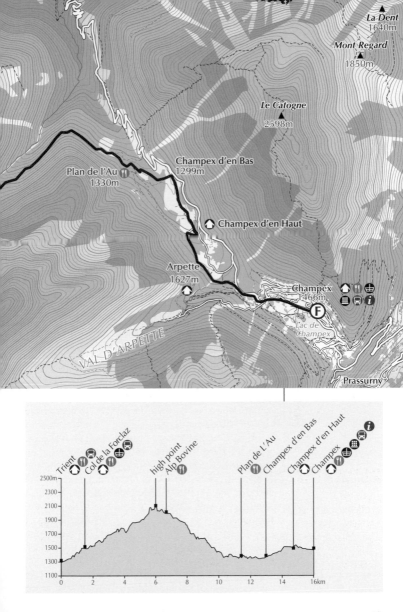

High on the Bovine route (photo: Madeline Williams)

Immediately over the col on the east side just beyond the shop, a sign to Alp Bovine points the way along the edge of a meadow beside buildings, then progresses on the top edge of a sloping pasture before twisting in and out of woodland and gaining height with views into the Rhône valley. Working a way round the **Combe des Faces**, in just over 1hr 30min come to a junction of paths (1725m) where you continue ahead, still rising across the wooded hillside.

After about 2hr the way passes to the left of a group of alp buildings (**La Giète** 1884m) in an open grass basin, beyond which the path resumes in larch- and pinewoods. Shortly after a short contouring section that gives direct views onto Martigny, the trail rises to a **high point** (2049m) on the edge of woodland (2hr 30 min) from which the buildings of Alp Bovine can be seen a short distance ahead. The way now eases down the slope to reach **Alp Bovine** (1987m, 2hr 45min, refreshments, emergency accommodation only).

The alp buildings are just to the left of the path in a gentle slope of pasture with views north-east along the Rhône valley. The trail (also used by the TMB) now descends slightly from Alp Bovine, and continues to zig-zag down to Plan de l'Au.

The rough sloping pastures of La Jure (with excellent bilberries in late summer) are crossed about 1hr beyond Alp Bovine, then you descend an open slope to a track which eases round the hillside and brings you to the farm buildings of **Plan l'Au** (1330m, 4hr 10min, refreshments) which has a small *buvette* (refreshment hut). From here the track becomes a narrow metalled road, but 2min beyond the farm you break off to the right on a signed path which rises to woodland.

When the path forks in the forest take the left branch. Soon pass below a group of chalets and come to a road at **Champex d'en Bas** (1299m, 4hr 30min). Turn right, pass the strung-out houses of this little village and at the upper end at a minor crossroads turn right over the bridge. The road once again becomes a track and climbs steadily, passing a sign to Auberge de Bon Abri. In 5hr come to **Champex d'en Haut**.

Looking back to the Dents du Midi from the Bovine route (photo: Madeline Williams)

The tranquil Champex Lac

CHAMPEX D'EN HAUT (1440m) Accommodation at Auberge-Gîte Bon Abri for 57 people, open all year (tel 027 783 14 23, **www.gite-bonabri.com**); Hôtel-Club Sunways (tel 027 783 11 22, **www. sunways.ch**).

About 300 metres beyond Hôtel Sunways join the main valley road and turn right, rising to a high point at 1498m, then sloping downhill with the snow-crowned Grand Combin seen ahead, and come to **Champex** (5hr 45min).

CHAMPEX (1466m) Accommodation (hotels, pensions, dortoirs, camping), restaurants, shops, PTT, bus link with Orsières and Martigny. Tourist information: **www.champex.info**. Lower-priced accommodation: Ptarmigan (B&B), 6 places, open all year (tel 027 783 16 40); Pension En Plein Air, 61 places in dortoirs/beds, suitable for budget group accommodation, open mid-January to the end of September (tel 027 783 23 50, **www. pensionenpleinair.ch**).

STAGE 4
Champex – Sembrancher – Le Châble

Start	Champex (1466m)
Distance	14.5km
Total ascent	200m
Total descent	840m
Time	4hr 15min
Low point	Sembrancher (712m)
Accommodation	Sembrancher (2hr 15min): hotels; Le Châble: hotels, pension, B&B
Transport options	Bus (Champex–Orsières); train (Orsières–Sembrancher–Le Châble)

Leaving Champex the route departs from that of the Tour of Mont Blanc and footpaths will be less busy. On this stage a gentle downhill walk followed by a pleasant valley stroll makes a good cushion between two strenuous days. Although there are no passes to cross and no big glacier-hung mountains close at hand, it is by no means a dull day, for the path takes you into an everyday working Switzerland – a Switzerland that rarely appears in tourist brochures, but which nevertheless is good to see. There are small farming communities along the way, patches of hillside being cultivated far from chocolate-box resorts, and all with a general air of pastoral well-being.

If you were so inclined, Le Châble could be reached in a morning's walk. But there's little to gain by rushing, for the onward route to Cabane du Mont Fort is too far to be achieved on top of this stage. Take the opportunity to enjoy a leisurely amble down to Sembrancher, and from there stroll into Val de Bagnes and make the most of your time.

Wander through Champex village heading south-east alongside the **lake**, and at the far end take the road branching left, signed to Hotels Belvedere, Splendide and Alpina. Rounding a dog-leg bend you come to the end of the road at Hotel Alpina. A few paces beyond the hotel at a junction of paths, take the right-hand option, signed to

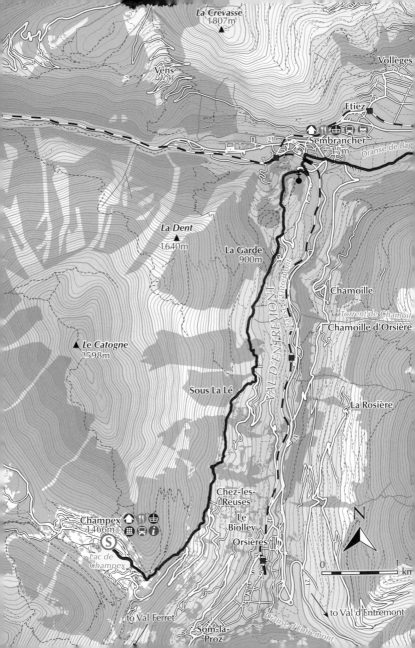

Sembrancher. Descending into woods it loses height with a steady gradient. Keeping straight ahead at all junctions you will come onto a gravel track which takes you above the hamlet of **Chez-les-Reuses** (1158m).

Do not descend to the hamlet but continue straight ahead following the yellow path signs, joining another track coming from the right and soon cutting into a cleft above a small gorge. When it forks take the lower, right-hand branch which goes round pastureland, and you will come to another fork, where this time you take the left-hand option. Before long come to a T-junction of trails; bear left and 15 metres later slant away to the right on a waymarked grass track signed to Sous La Lé, La Garde and Sembrancher. This brings you down to a gravel farm road above the small village of **Sous La Lé** (Soulalex on some maps, 1hr 10min).

Walk down to the village, and then bear left at a water trough and wander along a narrow street that leads to a junction of roads where you continue straight ahead, but instead of descending to a group of houses, take the left-hand track signposted to La Garde. Keep to the main, upper track when a choice is given, until a second track junction is reached immediately after crossing a partially hidden stream. Continue ahead, now easing downhill among pastures to a junction of four tracks (Tetou). Go straight ahead on a path descending among trees, branching left at an intersection, and soon arrive in the village of **La Garde** (900m, 1hr 40min).

In the village pass a chapel on your right and walk along a street in the direction of St-Jean and Sembrancher, then down to a crosstracks (Le Creux) where you go straight ahead, soon reaching a hairpin bend in a road. Once more continue ahead on a track again signed to St-Jean and Sembrancher, following power lines. Between here and Sembrancher there are various footpath alternatives, with directions indicated at all route junctions. The most direct waymarked trail is that which passes to the left of the little chapel of St-Jean and descends through woodland, goes beneath a railway line and brings you into **Sembrancher** (2hr 15min).

SEMBRANCHER (717m) Accommodation, refreshments, shop, PTT, Postbus and railway.

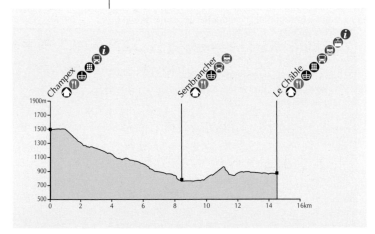

The narrow cobbled streets of Sembrancher (photo: Madeline Williams)

Hôtel-Restaurant de la Gare (tel 027 785 11 14); Office du Tourisme (tel 027 785 12 23).

As you begin to enter the village, take the right turn signed to Le Châble next to a water fountain, and continue straight ahead in an easterly direction, soon crossing the main road to continue straight ahead between chalets. ▶

If you wish to explore this quiet stone-walled village with its attractive little square, continue down the street past the water fountain.

VAL DE BAGNES

Rising in an attractive cirque of mountains rimmed by the Swiss-Italian border south-east of the Grand Combin, the Val de Bagnes contains a diverse set of landscapes: from open tarn-flecked pastures to deep gorge-like defiles, and from bleak screes and seemingly barren moraines to forests and meadows full of flowers. There are several remote mountain huts, challenging trails and a number of walkers' passes, all of which make this a splendid base for a walking holiday – see *Walking in the Valais* by Kev Reynolds (Cicerone Press). Despite the fact that the valley is sparsely populated with only a few hamlets and even fewer villages, the Val de Bagnes commune is Switzerland's largest, and at 295km^2 is greater in extent than the cantons of Geneva, Schaffhausen and Zug.

The narrow tarmac road goes between low-lying pastures and fields with encouraging views ahead. When you come to a fork near a wooden cross take the left branch ahead. At another fork near a small fenced building, take the right branch on what is now a track, and wander up into forest.

Having gained height in the forest the track forks. Take the lower option, signed to Le Châble, and soon after break off on a waymarked footpath descending to the left. At the foot of the slope come onto a track at a hairpin bend. Go round this hairpin to the left and onto another track – the Promenade de la Dranse (3hr). Keeping to the south side of the river, wander ahead alongside the **Dranse de Bagnes**, eventually coming to a narrow metalled road leading to the main road at a bridge. Do not cross the river but follow the road past several municipal buildings, then branch left on the narrow track between meadows heading towards the church at **Le Châble** (4hr 15min).

Evening in the valley community of Le Châble

LE CHÂBLE (821M)

Huddled on the left (west) bank of the Dranse de Bagnes, Le Châble is the valley capital, while its neighbour just across the bridge on the east side of the river is the more modern 'suburb' of Villette. Le Châble's village square has a very French appearance, but some of the old stone-walled farmhouses in the back streets pronounce their Valaisian authenticity by displaying over their doorways the horns of long-deceased cattle that have taken part in cow fights (*Combats de Reines*), a purely local (Valaisian) tradition. cablecar access with Verbier starts just across the river next to the railway station – Le Châble is the valley terminus of a branch line of the St Bernard Express which begins in Martigny. From the village a Postbus service runs upvalley (July–September only) as far as the huge Mauvoisin dam, from where walkers and climbers set out on a 4hr trek to the Chanrion hut. The Cabane de Louvie can be reached from the village of Fionnay and a 2hr ascent.

Accommodation, restaurants, shops, banks, PTT, Postbus and cableway to Verbier, train to Martigny. Further information from: Office du Tourisme, 1934 Le Châble (tel 027 775 38 70, **www.verbier.ch**). Lower-priced accommodation: Hôtel La Poste (tel 076 439 10 10); and in Villette across the river: Hôtel du Gietroz (tel 027 776 11 84) and Restaurant L'Escale (tel 027 776 27 07).

The Grand Combin, seen from the path between the Col Termin and the Col de Louvie

ROUTING TO AND AFTER THE CABANE DU MONT FORT

It is common for trekkers to take the cablecar from Le Châble to Les Ruinettes and then walk the 1hr 15min to the Cabane du Mont Fort, although this is to miss out on a stage that is much better than expected, with restaurants and views of the Combin and back to the Mont Blanc range. There is ample time to take the cablecar after the walk to Le Châble in one day, but valley hotels at Le Châble may provide one-day passes that allow the lift to be used at no charge.

For those who take the cablecar in the morning, tackling the route onwards to Prafleuri gives a very long day and is only for the toughest mountain walkers. An alternative, described as Stage 5A would be to walk the Sentier des Chamois to Col Termin and then descend to the Cabane de Louvie (in 4–4hr 30min), a charming refuge in an idyllic spot. The following day either reclimb to Col Termin or take a more direct trail to Col de Louvie. This would cut the walking time of the hard Stage 6 to the Cabane de Prafleuri by an hour.

In recent years stonefall above and onto the Sentier des Chamois after the Cabane du Mont Fort caused the Valais authorities to redesignate this path as a blue path, an Alpine route. As a walk, little has actually changed and it remains both viable and our main route for the Haute Route trekker.

As the main alternative over the Col de la Chaux is also an Alpine route, independent trekkers who wish to avoid blue paths have some planning to do. Also, groups led by walking leaders (as opposed to full mountain guides) may have insurance issues on these Alpine paths.

The options to get round this are:

1   Take a lower path running below and then climbing to the Sentier des Chamois before Col Termin. This involves an extra net 400m of ascent and descent and adds an hour to the Col Termin walk. The path may be safer from rockfall, but in its current state is a less attractive route, and adds time to the already long day to Prafleuri.

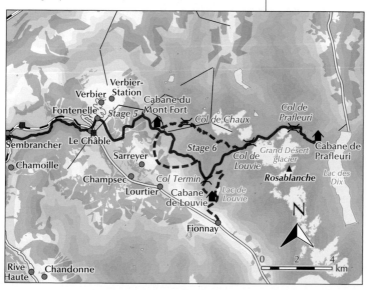

91

2   Take a bus from Sembrancher (or Le Châble) to
     Fionnay in the Val de Bagnes. From here it is a steep
     2hr climb to the Cabane de Louvie from where you
     gain the Col Termin or the Col de Louvie by more
     direct routes, cutting an hour from the stage to
     Prafleuri.

So, having explored all options, our judgement is
that Cabane du Mont Fort and the Sentier des Chamois
are the preferred routing for most trekkers. Besides, sunset and sunrise over the Mont Blanc range are wonderful.

STAGE 5

Le Châble – Clambin – Cabane du Mont Fort

Start	Le Châble (821m)
Distance	13km
Total ascent	1660m
Total descent	20m
Time	5hr 30min
High point	Cabane du Mont Fort (2457m)
Accommodation	Cabane du Mont Fort: SAC refuge
Transport options	Postbus (Le Châble–Verbier); cableway (Le Châble–Verbier–Les Ruinettes)

A first glance at the map gives little indication that a walking route can be
made between Val de Bagnes and Cabane du Mont Fort without extensive
use of either the steeply twisting road to Verbier or the lengthy zig-zag road
from Lourtier through Sarreyer.

But there is a route, and a delightful one at that. It's a combination of
narrow lanes, tracks and footpaths – often steeply climbing, but always
interesting. There are some fine villages, an attractive chapel, long forest
sections with welcome shade on a hot day, high pastures and some truly
magnificent views. With so much height to gain it is advisable to make an
early start, take your time and enjoy everything the ascent has to offer. But
before setting out you should telephone ahead to reserve bed-space for the

night at Cabane du Mont Fort – the number is given at the end of the route details.

This walk avoids Verbier altogether in an effort to remain as far from mechanisation as possible. It's impossible to escape all sign of the downhill ski industry, however, for Verbier and its surrounding hillsides offer a winter paradise for the skier, and an abundance of lifts and cableways have effectively laced the mountains like an old-fashioned corset. This is especially true around the Cabane du Mont Fort. This may put some walkers off – if so continue to the Cabane de Louvie, which also has great views. But the sunrise and sunset at Mont Fort are second to none, with the Mont Blanc and Combin ranges dominating the horizon and many will think this full compensation.

It is on this stage that the Grand Combin begins to exert its influence. This great snowy massif dominates the Val de Bagnes (and, to an extent, Val d'Entremont too). It's the most westerly 4000m mountain of the Pennine Alps, an attractive, substantial block that cultivates a number of glaciers and whose presence is recognised for several days yet to come. Although the walk does not stray to it, the Combin nevertheless imposes its personality on the Haute Route trekker with its sheer size and grandeur. Since leaving Mont Blanc (whose bulk was always behind you) the Combin massif is the first on the walk to impress with such authority and grace.

▶ From Le Châble cross the river to **Villette** and turn left. Initially the route is part of the Tour des Villages, and is waymarked with yellow diamonds or stripes outlined in black. Turn right after Café-Restaurant La Ruinette and follow waymarks up through the village along narrow streets, passing houses and dark timber granaries, some of which are perched on staddle stones. In 10min cross the Villette–Verbier road by Café Magnin and enter **Le Cotterg** (880m). A currently unclear signpost after 50 metres directs you to the right to Chapelle les Verneys in 50min (ignore the sign straight ahead up the hill to Cabane du Mont Fort, as this goes via Verbier). This turn in Le Cotterg is probably the critical turn of the whole stage and is easily missed. Once made, the route falls easily into place. If missed, you are on your way to

Should you decide that the steep uphill route to Cabane du Mont Fort is not for you, an easy option is to take the cableway from Le Châble to Verbier, and from there to Les Ruinettes at 2195m. From there a signed track-then-path leads to the Mont Fort hut in 1hr 15min.

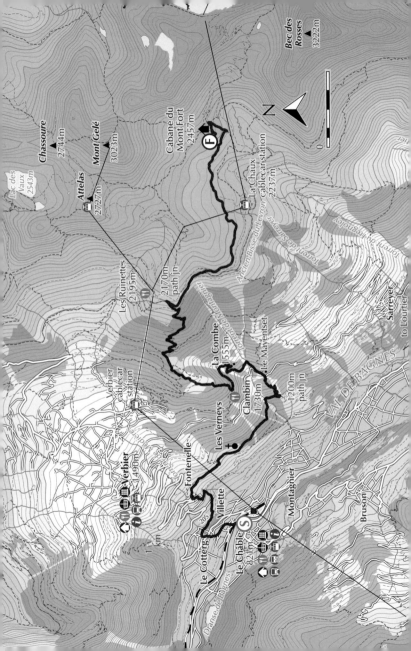

Verbier. With waymarks and signposts as your guide, a series of tracks and footpaths lead to **Fontenelle**.

As you come to this hamlet, dug into the steep hillside, take a narrow footpath breaking away beside a wooden cross (dated 1982) to edge alongside an orchard (1045m, 30min), or explore the old wooden houses in the hamlet. An unmetalled road takes you round the hillside heading south-east, and eventually brings you to the small but elegant white chapel and few buildings of **Les Verneys** (1120m, 1hr, water supply, public toilets).

Continue beyond the buildings for about 5min, and when the track makes a sharp right-hand bend and descends, take a signed footpath ahead leading uphill. This goes into forest, gaining height steeply at times in order to cross a scoop in the mountainside. This 'scoop' opens to a combe higher up. Crossing a stream the way climbs on, but having gained a high point you then descend a few metres to a junction of paths (1200m, 1hr 20min and 20min from Les Verneys). This is **Le Mayentset**. Turn left, climbing steeply in forest on

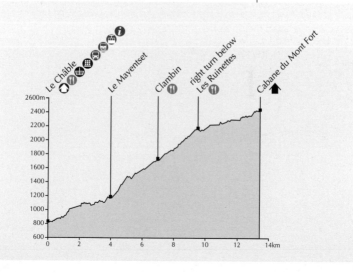

a path signed to Les Ruinettes and Clambin, with yellow and black waymarks.

This trail rises quite steeply on the right-hand (south) side of what soon becomes a distinctive combe and leads to a handful of timber buildings, above which you bear left on an unmetalled road, and when it forks soon after, take the upper track. This winds uphill in long loops with waymarked footpath shortcuts.

The footpath leads up to a pair of wooden buildings (La Combe 1555m) and passes between them. A few paces beyond these the path forks (this may not be very clear). Take the lower option across the hillside pasture, re-enter forest and continue for some way to a footpath junction at 1600m, where you bear right on a rising trail signed to Clambin and Les Ruinettes. (The path straight ahead at this junction goes to Verbier.) It's a steep ascent, but when you come out of forest to a small open patch of pasture, there's a wonderful view of the Combin massif on the far side of Val de Bagnes. This is the first of many magnificent sightings, but the magic never fades.

Mont Blanc range from Le Clambin

Continue towards a stone-based chalet, but veer left before it and pass beside a timber chalet with Verbier seen below in a large grassy basin. An easy path then brings you to a junction of tracks at **Clambin** (1730m,

The restaurant at Clambin looks west towards the Mont Blanc massif

THE COMBIN MASSIF

The large and impressive Combin massif has several distinct summits over 4000m. Standing entirely in Switzerland the summit crown has a splay of ridges from which busy glacial systems pour down; the largest being the great Glacier de Corbassière which falls in a series of terraces to the north, and is the largest icefield in the Western Pennine Alps. (A fine close view of these icy terraces is to be had from Cabane de Panossière, reached by a 4hr walk from Fionnay.)

Although several ascents were made of a secondary peak (Aiguille du Croissant) in 1857–58, the actual summit of Grand Combin (Combin de Graffeneire, 4314m) was first climbed on 30 July 1859 by Charles St-Claire Deville, with the guides Daniel, Emmanuel and Gaspard Balleys and Basile Dorsaz. Nowadays the massif attracts ski-mountaineers as well as summer-season climbers, and is frequently traversed by those tackling the winter Haute Route on ski.

3hr, refreshments) – an attractive restaurant which enjoys a wonderful panorama is seen a short distance to the left. There's a water supply nearby. Go right, then immediately left on a track signed to Les Ruinettes and Cabane du Mont Fort.

VERBIER

One of the best-known ski resorts in the Alps, Verbier sprawls within a large natural basin of hillside high above the valley, a real sun-trap and an obvious site for development as a ski village since the amphitheatre that cradles it holds plenty of snow and the slopes are ideal for skiers of all standards. It has an over-abundance of mechanical lifts – 80 or so, if you include those in the neighbouring Val de Nendaz which is easily accessible from it. Thanks to the great ski boom of the 1960s, the original village of Verbier has been swamped by a rash of chalets, hotels and unattractive apartment blocks, but many footpaths lead from it to take the eager walker into scenes of peace and tranquility. For information contact: Office du Tourisme, 1936 Verbier (tel 027 775 38 88, www.verbier.ch).

This track rises to another junction (Hatay, 1844m), where you bear right and a few paces later slant left uphill and come to a picnic/barbecue area marked as Le Hattey (1860m, water supply). A piste has been bulldozed down the hillside above Le Hattey; at first the path follows the piste for several turns, before a sign takes you right, still climbing in forest, until you emerge at last to spectacular views of the Grand Combin and the Mont Blanc massif beyond intervening ridges in the south-west.

Emerge at a **junction** (2170m, 4hr 15min) 25m vertical and less than half a kilometre below the cablecar station at Les Ruinettes (2195m). On coming to a track by a cableway pylon (5hr 15min from Le Châble) turn

On this upward path we came upon an elderly Swiss couple descending. They wore smiles as bright as their red shirts and were so obviously enjoying their day out that we stopped to speak and shared with them a love of the morning, of the near views and far, and talked briefly of other mountains and valleys, of huts and villages, of glaciers and snowfields and birdsong and the fragrance of the forest – in general feeding off each other's enthusiasm. Then the lady whispered that her husband could now only walk up the gentlest of hills – but he'd swallowed his pride and taken the occasional chairlift or cablecar to enable him to reach the loftier view-points from which he was happy to walk down. 'Well,' she confided, 'he is 82.' With that my prejudices stacked against cableways in the mountains came crashing down around me.

right along it. Before long this rises as a path, and at a signed junction continues alongside a *bisse* to a dirt road. Cross this road to another narrow path which rises in a few paces to join another *bisse*. ▶ Follow the *bisse* path on an easy contour round the hillside leading to a junction of trails below the knoll on which stands **Cabane du Mont Fort** (5hr 30min).

CABANE DU MONT FORT (2457m) 58 places, meals and drinks available, open end of June

There are wonderful views still to the Grand Combin and its neighbouring peaks and glaciers drawing you on.

Cabane du Mont Fort

*Looking west from the
Cabane du Mont Fort*

to mid-September, (tel 027 778 13 84, **www.
cabanemontfort.ch**). Owned by the Jaman Section
of the Swiss Alpine Club, this hut is superbly placed
on a bluff due south of Mont Gelé and is understandably popular with C–Z trekkers (advance
booking advised). There are several high passes
within easy reach, including Col de Chassoure, Col
du Mont Gelé, Col des Gentianes, Col de la Chaux
and Col Termin, which are all crossed by walkers in
summer. Unfortunately a spider's web of cableways
has devalued some of these passes, but others hap-
pily remain free from mechanisation. Despite ski
lifts and farm tracks below, views from the hut are
splendid, with Grand Combin and the Mont Blanc
massif taking pride of place, but the Dents du Midi
are also on show. Sunsets are magnificent.

STAGE 5A

Le Châble (Les Ruinettes) –
Col Termin – Cabane de Louvie

Start	Le Châble (Les Ruinettes)
Distance	10km
Total ascent	640m (and 1350m by cablecar)
Total descent	600m
Time	4hr
High point	Col Termin (2648m)
Accommodation	Cabane du Mont Fort (1hr 15min); Cabane de Louvie (4hr)
Transport options	cablecar from Le Châble to Les Ruinettes cablecar station
Continuation	The route rejoins the Stage 6 route about 30min after Col Termin, 2km, 1hr 15min and +440m from the Cabane de Louvie

This alternative staging passes by the Cabane du Mont Fort and overnights at the attractive Cabane de Louvie. It takes in the balcony views from the Sentier des Chamois and cuts the walking on the long stage to Cabane de Prafleuri by an hour and would suit those who wish to minimise the sight of ski-infrastructure. A strong walker might walk the route in an afternoon after the descent from Champex, or even continue on after the Stage 5 climb to the Cabane du Mont Fort; but both would be long days. Better to stay in Le Châble and use the lift – a voucher from a hotel in Le Châble currently provides a free lift to Les Ruinettes.

The stage takes in the high-level *bisse* path to Mont Fort, as well as the Sentier des Chamois, with magnificent views to the Combin range.

▶ Start from the Les Ruinettes cablecar station. The *bisse* path starts 250m below the station, although alternative marked tracks are available, if less attractive. Follow the route described in Stage 5 as far as the **Cabane du Mont Fort** (2457m, 1hr 15min).

For route map see Stage 6.

From the Cabane du Mont Fort follow the main route described in Stage 6 following signs for the **Col Termin** (2648m, 3hr 15min). Parties who wish or need to avoid the blue Alpine path can use the lower, less attractive route that joins the Sentier after 2hr 20min, and adds an hour to the stage (see Stage 6 alternative). Views to the Combin are best earlier in the day as clouds may gather and the mountain is directly to the south.

From Col Termin the Lac de Louvie and its hut are seen far below. Take the signed route dropping steeply to the **Cabane de Louvie** (4hr).

> **CABANE DE LOUVIE (2207m)** privately owned, 54 dortoir places, 4 double rooms, tel 027 778 17 40. Located above the Lac de Louvie, the hut is splendidly sited with views across the depths of the Val de Bagnes to the Combin.

Alternative ascent to the Cabane de Louvie from Fionnay

If you face bad weather and the higher route is best left alone, or if you need to reach the Cabane de Louvie on the same day you leave Champex, then it can be reached by a direct ascent from Fionnay. Take the postbus to

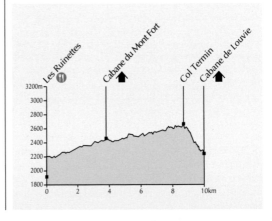

Cabane de Louvie

Fionnay from Sembrancher or Le Châble (limited service). (The valley walk from Le Châble is possible but if walking it would be better to take the high route described above.)

The climbs starts from the bus stop. Leave the remarkably ugly apartment building to your right, continue along a raised ledge above the road for 100 metres and then turn right, climbing to a path junction where you turn left. The path climbs in steady but steep loops before turning a corner round a descending ridge. After this it becomes rougher and is protected by cables in places, looking down into the impressive gorge below. It levels as you approach the dam wall, and the **Cabane de Louvie** is just above you on the left. It takes 2hr to climb the 720m to the hut.

The following morning rejoin the main route, either by returning to the Col Termin, or, more directly, taking a path alongside the Lac and climbing to a left turn at Plan de la Gole before a short steep path joins the main route at 2630m, 30min after Col Termin is passed on the main route (1hr 15min, 2km, +420m).

STAGE 6

*Cabane du Mont Fort – Col Termin – Col de
Louvie – Col de Prafleuri – Cabane de Prafleuri*

Start	Cabane du Mont Fort (2457m)
Distance	17km
Total ascent	1110m
Total descent	940m
Time	7hr 30min
High point	Col de Prafleuri (2987m)
Accommodation	Cabane de Prafleuri: mountain refuge; Hôtel-Restaurant du Barrage (1hr from Cabane de Prafleuri)
Transport options	None

This is a strenuous stage, with the crossing of 3½ cols (the 'false' Col de Prafleuri 40min before the real col can be a real dampener, so be prepared). The Grand Désert route below Rosablanche has evolved over many years and what was in the past a glacier crossing now traverses a vast wilderness of rock. It is reasonably waymarked but is a featureless area and under snow and/or in poor visibility would provide a significant navigational challenge. Take care as the precise routing may change.

The stage is full of variety and ever-changing views. At first there are vast panoramas, but as you wander along the high belvedere trail to Col Termin, so the Combin massif dominates the scene. If you walk quietly and remain alert, you stand a good chance of seeing ibex on or near the path (this is a noted wildlife sanctuary). Later, on the eastern side of Col de Louvie, you are faced with a bewildering landscape of dying glaciers, chaotic moraines and a seemingly barren wilderness. But even in such landscapes the majesty of the mountains impresses itself; yet one grows convinced (if you ever needed convincing) that the 'everlasting hills' are everlasting only in the words of the poet. On this walk you are witness to the ceaseless toil of erosion. The mountains are falling apart, and to wander through their scenes of destruction is a sobering experience.

Under normal summer conditions the walk should present no major route-finding difficulties, but in poor visibility, or under threat of storm, problems may arise on the Grand Désert stretch between Col de Louvie (2921m) and Col de Prafleuri (2987m), where there is no real path other than a trail of cairns and paint flashes. The Sentier des Chamois between Cabane du Mont Fort and Col Termin (classified as an 'Alpine route' with blue–white waymarks) is also one to avoid under icy conditions. Seek the advice of the guardian at Mont Fort in case of uncertainty. He may advise using the alternative route across Col de la Chaux as a safer option.

▶ Descend north-east from Cabane du Mont Fort to the major path junction where you turn right, and after a few metres branch left on a waymarked path that winds downhill to meet a track at a hairpin bend. Follow the track to the next (right-hand) hairpin, then break away on

The following route is a long and tiring stage – remember that the time quoted (7hr 30min) does not include rests, so it could take at least 9–10hr to get from one hut to the next. Fill your water bottle before setting out, and make sure you have food to sustain you on what could be the toughest day so far.

The options from Cabane du Mont Fort

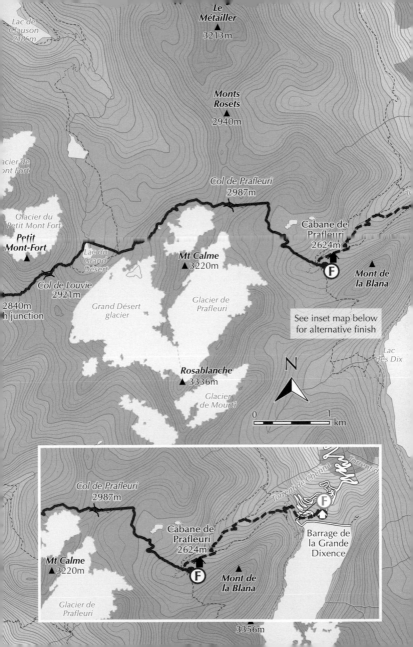

a narrow path signed with a blue sign heading across a basin of rocks and scree. It crosses a few minor streams, then makes a rising traverse of the slope ahead, where you turn a spur which marks the start of the **Sentier des Chamois**. With splendid views of the Combin massif, the *sentier* is narrow and exposed in places, but it makes a tremendous belvedere as you contour along the precipitous mountainside high above the Val de Bagnes.

Lower route from Cabane du Mont Fort

Using the red/white alternative path adds a further hour to the overall time for this stage, and in many respects is a less favoured option (7.5km to path junction; ascent 625m, descent 535m).

From Cabane du Mont Fort descend north-east to the major path junction where you turn right, and follow the broad path downhill signed to La Chaux and Col Termin. This path is well signed and designated with red and white paint splashes. The path descends steadily, and at a junction with a track turn right and descend until it joins another track just below the **La Chaux** cablecar station. Turn sharp left, and then fork right at a track junction, then just before a right-hand bend in the track take the signed path straight ahead, following this path as it

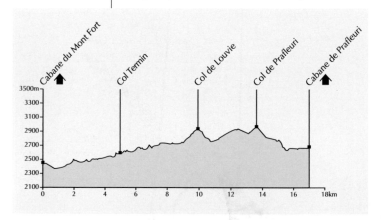

Morning light on the Mont Blanc range at the Cabane du Mort Fort (photo: Madeline Williams)

continues to descend to 2099m, then contours around the hillside to a **path junction at 2113m**. Turn left and start to climb, occasionally steeply with some exposed sections, before a final short section of tight zig-zags up a steep exposed hillside to reach the **Sentier des Chamois** at 2546m (2hr 20min).

After 1hr 20min from the hut you reach a junction where a trail descends to Le Mintset. Ignore this and continue straight ahead, keeping alert for signs of ibex or chamois. ▶

Views remain magnificent – Grand Combin aloof across the valley, and the Val de Bagnes itself a very long way beneath the trail. Views back to the north-west show the Dents du Midi in the distance.

We were finding the path difficult to negotiate. Not that there were obstacles in the way, nor were conditions at all bad. Neither were we bothered by the steep slopes plunging to Val de Bagnes 1500m below. Our problems arose from lack of concentration, for the glories of the Combin massif across the valley were so outstanding that our attention was being held by them – away from the first principle of safety on the path. It was difficult to take our eyes off that gleaming mass that had conjured a streamer of cloud just below the summit and was teasing as in a dance of the seven veils. The summit was clear, so were the lower slopes. But the midriff of the mountain was veiled. It was a tantalising view. Then, when we did correct our attention to review the way ahead, it was to spy a herd of 20 or so ibex moving in morning shadow below us. They were very close, and completely unconcerned by our presence.

The way then reaches the saddle of **Col Termin** (2648m, 2hr) in a shoulder of the Bec Termin which rises to the north. From here a very wild landscape rises to north and east, with Mont Fort and Rosablanche both casting out some high ridges to confuse.

> **Rosablanche** (3336m) offers easy ascent routes and a celebrated panorama from its summit – an exceptionally fine viewpoint from which to study larger peaks of the main Pennine chain. It is popular as a skiing expedition in spring, and from the Prafleuri hut for walkers in summer (2hr from the hut by way of the Prafleuri glacier). It was first climbed in September 1865.

Steeply below lies Lac de Louvie, with a hut above its southern end that enjoys one of the finest views in the Swiss Alps; worth remembering for a return visit to Val de Bagnes.

Descend on the east side for a few metres, then veer sharply left on the path signed to Col de Louvie and Prafleuri. ◄ About 15min from the col a path breaks away and descends to the lake and the Cabane de Louvie, but for the main route ignore this and continue towards a wild-looking rocky cirque at the head of the Louvie valley. A rough boulder tip is crossed, but after this the path improves. Views remain impressive.

After crossing a much larger boulder field, and at least 1-1hr 30min from Col Termin (timings are difficult to predict here in view of the roughness of the ground and difficulties if there is any snow), you reach a path junction where the left-hand option breaks away to Col de la Chaux and Mont Fort. Continue straight ahead, over another boulder field and, skirting the left-hand side of a narrow stony valley, you climb to gain the rocky **Col de Louvie** (2921m, 4hr).

Alternative route to the Col de Louvie by the Col de la Chaux

On this more direct, and therefore slightly shorter route to Col de Louvie, the Col de la Chaux is seen behind Cabane du Mont Fort at the head of a stony hanging valley. Although it is rough underfoot and without the wonderful views of the Sentier des Chamois – Col Termin

main route, the Col de la Chaux crossing is preferable and safer under certain conditions, although this is by no means an easy route, and can be very challenging in, for example, fresh snow. Should the guardian at Cabane du Mont Fort advise against using the Sentier des Chamois, this could be your best bet. Check locally for current conditions.

High on the Col de la Chaux with early morning snow, looking back to Mont Fort and the Vaudois Alps (photo: Madeline Williams)

This is a higher route than Col Termin, but saves 4km and about 1hr on a long and tiring stage. It joins the main Col Termin route 30min before reaching the Col de Louvie, and then crosses the Grand Désert to Prafleuri, so the cautionary notes about this post-glacialwilderness area apply in full.

Descend from Cabane du Mont Fort on an easy-angled track that winds into the stony basin to the east. As you enter the basin/hanging valley, note that there are two tracks pushing into it. Go to the upper track and follow this as it pushes upvalley on a ski piste to gain height. After about 50min come to a junction (2706m). The continuing track climbs to Col des Gentianes, but the Col de la Chaux path breaks away to the right.

The path, waymarked blue–white, picks a way across a very stony terrain and passes above a small glacial lake. It then steers onto the left-hand slope of the hanging valley, guided still by waymarks and cairns where the path is thin or non-existent. Do not be alarmed if you lose this path; continue carefully over the boulders towards the col and you will soon find waymarks again.

Soon gain the rocky **Col de la Chaux** (2940m, 1hr 45min) to exchange one desolate stony scene for another. Looking back you see beyond the coffee-coloured glacial tarn to Cabane du Mont Fort and the spiky Dents du Midi as a backdrop. Ahead lies another stony bowl, and across its bounding ridge the summit of Rosablanche can be seen with the Grand Désert glacier draped down its north-west face.

A steep descent path cuts left below the col, skirts the slopes of the basin then veers right (well waymarked) to cross a rocky shoulder from which the Grand Combin is once more on show. Here you find a **junction of paths at 2840m** (2hr 30min). The path right leads to Col Termin and the Cabane de Louvie, so turn left to climb to Col de Louvie.

A barren landscape greets you in the north-east – a wilderness of screes, moraine and the dying glacier spilling from Rosablanche. The Grand Désert is well named.

Take the Louvie path and follow the main route description for Stage 6 to gain **Col de Louvie** (2921m, 3hr). Both the Mont Blanc massif and Grand Combin can be seen when looking back from here. ◄

From the Col de Louvie the route descends a narrow, rocky little valley – again, well waymarked, although care is needed in places where there is no real path. As you lose height note a large red–white waymark painted on a boulder on the eastern side of the bowl ahead, beyond the Grand Désert glacier – this is a guide for later. Follow the immediate line of waymarks and occasional cairns that lead down to the outflow stream at the northern end of a glacial tarn (2760m, 4hr 30min) below the snout of the **Grand Désert**. Over this turn right and make your way initially south-east, then north-east up and across a vast stony wasteland to a line of cairns and waymarks. ◄

Both the LS 1:50,000 and Kümmerley + Frey 1:60,000 maps show an old path passing south of the tarn. This is no longer in use.

The route then climbs and takes you past a number of little tarns and glacial ponds, crossing broad granite slabs and jumbled boulders. Waymarks are frequent, but in poor visibility it is absolutely essential not to lose sight of them. Take compass bearings where necessary.

The route eventually levels out at the 'false col de Prafleuri' and the real Col de Prafleuri is seen at the head of what looks like a steep slope of scree, and is in fact boulders. A small glacier flows down from Grand Mont Calme west of the pass, and the waymarked trail brings you to its edge, where it is necessary to descend a short but steep and broken slope (sometimes snow or ice) in order to continue to the foot of the pass. Descend with care – a frustrating descent, for you have to climb again to reach the pass.

The climb to the col can be tiring, as it involves working a way up a steepish slope of rough blocks, scree

Looking across the Grand Désert, a post-glacial wilderness of rock and water (photo: Madeline Williams)

Cabane de Prafleuri, a privately owned hut with good facilities

and scattered rocks, but at last (and no doubt with relief) you arrive at the **Col de Prafleuri** (2987m, 6hr 15min) to be greeted by a view south-east over a much-scarred and depressingly barren mountain bowl, with views to Mont Blanc de Cheilon, which dominates much of Stage 7.

Descend the steep path winding down to a level section beneath the Glacier de Prafleuri. Cross levelled gravel beds to a track where you bear right, soon leaving this on a waymarked footpath that drops to the left into a grim-looking valley where you descend steeply with a first sighting of **Cabane de Prafleuri**. The path takes you below the hut, so that the final approach is unfortunately up a short but steep path that deposits you at the door (7hr 30min).

CABANE DE PRAFLEURI (2624m) 59 places, manned from mid-March to end of April, and early July to mid-September, with a full meals service (tel 027 281 17 80, listed on the Valais accommodation website). Privately owned, the original Cabane de Prafleuri was constructed in the mid-1950s when quarrying work began below the Prafleuri glacier as

part of the Grande Dixence hydro-electric scheme.
(The hut was used to house site-workers in the early
days.) While it lacks any views of inspiration, it is
particularly well sited for walkers on the Chamonix–
Zermatt route, for immediately above it to the south
the easy Col des Roux gives access to Val des Dix.
Ibex often approach the hut in the evening. (There
is also a bizarrely ugly but functional hotel at the
foot of the Dix Barrage, 1hr from Prafleuri.)

Route to the hotel at the base of the Dix Barrage

Instead of taking the final short steep path to the Cabane
de Prafleuri, take the broad path next to the stream. The
path gently descends, keeping to the east side of the torrent. At a path junction keep left downhill and continue
down on the east bank next to the stream. Ignore a path
joining from the left, but when the path divides (1.6km),
take the right fork which rises steadily to reach a high
point (2433m). From here, either drop on a small winding
path towards a farm building, then continue to descend
on a further zig-zag path that emerges just below a cablecar station. Alternatively descend to join a track which
initially heads south-east away from the barrage, but then
comes to a hairpin with excellent views of the lake and
Mont Blanc de Cheilon, before descending to the barrage and cablecar station. From here follow the signed
path which descends sometimes steeply to reach a small
chapel, and the hotel just below.

To rejoin Stage 7 the next day, climb to the dam and
continue on the track alongside the lake

STAGE 7

*Cabane de Prafleuri – Col des Roux
– Pas de Chèvres – Arolla*

Start	Cabane de Prafleuri (2624m)
Distance	18km
Total ascent	740m
Total descent	1360m
Time	6hr
High point	Pas de Chèvres 2855m or Col de Riedmatten (2919m)
Accommodation	Refuge des Ecoulaies (50min): unmanned mountain refuge; Refuge de la Gentiane La Barma (1hr): unmanned mountain refuge; Arolla: hotels, dortoirs, camping
Transport options	Bus (Le Chargeur–Vex); postbus (Vex–Arolla)

The walk that leads from the rather gloomy Prafleuri glen to Arolla is a true delight. Given fine weather conditions the views on this stage will be among the very best of all. There's the surprise vision that greets you on arrival at the first col of the day (Col des Roux), for you emerge from morning shadow to the incredible sight of the Val des Dix spread before you – a 5km lake, green pastures and big mountains. Best of all these mountains is the great pyramid-shaped Mont Blanc de Cheilon; but it has its handsome neighbours too, and as the day progresses so you draw closer to them, crossing the Pas de Chèvres or the Col de Riedmatten to descend beside Pigne d'Arolla, then below Mont Collon. Col de Riedmatten is a revelation – a rocky cleft in the Monts Rouges ridge from which you have a first view of the Matterhorn far off. (Make the most of it for you'll not see it again until you approach Zinal on Stage 10.)

Boulderfields below the Col de Riedmatten make this part of the route strenuous, but the path has been improved over recent years and it is much easier than it has been, although the final stretch is on loose and bouldery terrain. The 20–25m of ladders of the Pas de Chèvres, much improved in 2016, are arguably shorter and more straightforward than the col. Take care also as a rerouting several years ago at the Pas du Chat just after the Lac de Dix is not reflected on some maps.

An alternative via Cabane des Dix diverges from the main route after the Pas du Chat and also makes a very fine route, with the opportunity to break the walk with an overnight stay in a high mountain environment, set dramatically below the great north face of Mont Blanc de Cheilon. Both options have much to commend them, but the main route is quicker and more direct. The Dix alternative requires a short glacier crossing (no gear needed), the routing of which has moved south in recent years, lengthening the route and leaving a longer scramble below the Pas de Chèvres, so allow at least an extra hour on the direct route.

A signpost outside Cabane de Prafleuri indicates the start of the route to Col des Roux. There are also large painted signs on rocks and, where no actual path exists, sufficient waymarks keep you on track. Col des Roux is an obvious pass seen to the south of the hut and only 180m above it. The route is by way of a slope cluttered with rocks, but after an initial boulder tip, a good path leads to the col in easy zig-zags. In fact the ascent is achieved quickly and a lot more easily than might be imagined from below, and you come onto **Col des Roux** (2804m) in about 30min, to be rewarded by a view almost guaranteed to stop you in your tracks.

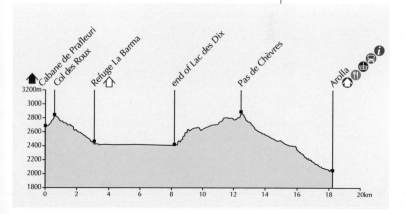

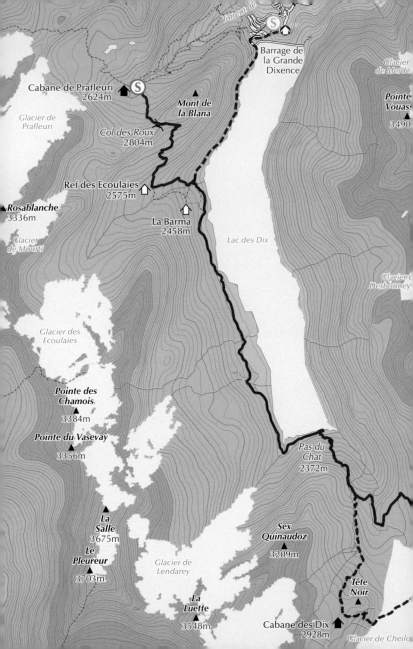

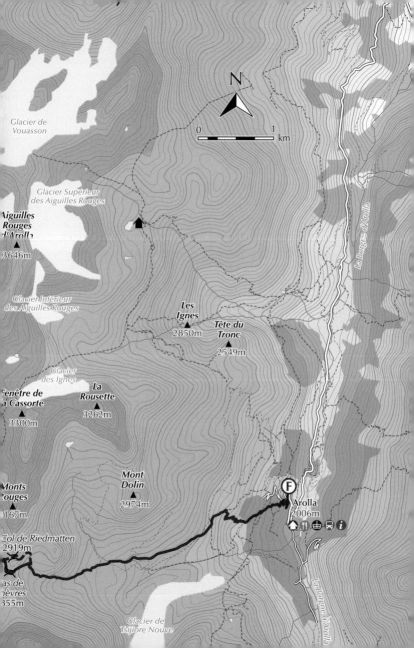

N

0   1
km

Glacier de
Vouasson

Glacier Supérieur
des Aiguilles Rouges

Aiguilles
Rouges
d'Arolla
3646m

Glacier Intérieur
des Aiguilles Rouges

Les
Ignes
2850m

Tête du
Tronc
2549m

Glacier
des Ignes

Fenêtre de
a Cassorte

La
Rousette
3262m

3300m

Monts
Rouges
167m

Mont
Dolin
2974m

F

Arolla
2006m

Col de Riedmatten
2919m

as de
ièvres
355m

Glacier de
Tsijiore Nouve

la Borgne d'Arolla

la Borgne d'Arolla

On the south side descend on a good trail that brings you to more boulders but then becomes easier underfoot. As you veer south-west into the pastures of a shallow valley below the Glacier des Ecoulaies, you can see the solitary building of the **Refuge des Ecoulaies** (50min).

> **REFUGE DES ECOULAIES (2575m)** is owned by the Ski Club des Pyramides (Euseigne). It has 22 places and is usually manned at weekends in summer; self-catering facilities only. For reservations tel 079 339 12 46 (**www.lespyramides.ch**).

The path descends directly between two streams to the Dix track. If you want to visit Refuge de la Gentiane La Barma, take the path which aims towards the refuge then forks. Take the left branch which crosses several streams, then descend to a glacial torrent with a footbridge. Over this the way eases round the hillside and brings you to another junction by the stone-built **Refuge de la Gentiane La Barma** (1hr).

> **REFUGE DE LA GENTIANE LA BARMA (2458m)** This privately owned hut is permanently open, but not always manned. It has places for about 50 and self-catering facilities (take your own stove). For enquiries and/or reservations tel 079 869 70 17 or 079 847 11 18. If you do use the facilities, please

Refuge de la Gentiane La Barma in Val des Dix

treat them with respect and do nothing to abuse the hospitality offered.

Overlooking Lac des Dix the **Refuge de la Gentiane La Barma** was originally part of a cheese dairy built in 1934 alongside cowsheds. When the dairy was abandoned in 1964, the buildings were acquired by the Gymnastic Society, La Gentiane, of Mâche (downvalley in Val d'Hérémence), which renovated them to create this delightful refuge.

Take the path ahead which passes just to the left of the refuge, and cross a meadow to join a farm track which you follow downhill to a hairpin bend. A signed path strikes ahead, then descends to a broad track running along the west side of **Lac des Dix**. Bear right and walk upvalley. With little effort required you can swing along with all senses alert to the wonders of the day, with marmots whistling from the trackside pastures, the clang of cowbells matching your stride, streams spilling down the hillsides, and snowgleam topping the peaks ahead.

Looking beyond the Barrage de la Grande Dixence, the Bernese Alps are seen in the distance

LAC DES DIX

Created as part of the Grande Dixence hydro-scheme that harnesses the waters of several Valaisian valleys, Lac des Dix is blocked at its northern end by the massive dam known as the Barrage de la Grande Dixence. At 284m the dam is claimed to be the world's highest. It's an impressive piece of engineering; from its base to the crest of the wall it stands twice as tall as the largest of Egypt's pyramids. It consists of 5,960,000m^3 of concrete and holds back some 400 million m^3 of water. The Grand Dixence scheme has a number of dams, all linked by service tunnels and feeder pipes.

About 20 metres before the track ends at a point known as the **Pas du Chat** (2372m, 2hr 15min), a sign indicates a path climbing steeply to the right. **Old maps and old editions of guidebooks show the route crossing the glacial river here. This is no longer the signed way (and looks rather dangerous).** The path mounts a slope of grass and rock, and continues for some time, climbing relentlessly before easing to the start of a rib of lateral moraine. Ascend this moraine to come to a signpost at about 2630m (45min or so from the Pas du Chat) directing to the Col de Riedmatten/Arolla route to the left. (The way to Cabane des Dix continues along the moraine crest.)

The shapely **Mont Blanc de Cheilon** (3870m) dominates the Val des Dix and towers over Cabane des Dix. Generally reckoned to be the finest peak in the Arolla district for rock and ice routes, it received its first ascent in September 1865 by the west-north-west flank, which is reached from the Col de Cheilon, now the normal route today.

Go down the left-hand path and in another 5min or so you cross a footbridge over the stream draining the Cheilon glacier, which is receding at an alarming rate. The way now cuts across glacial silt and moraine debris, then winds up the rock-strewn slope towards the Col de Riedmatten and Pas de Chèvres. ◀ The Dix hut is clearly seen across the Glacier de Cheilon. Waymarks guide you

In poor visibility this is a tricky area – do not allow yourself to be misled by the blue signs to the difficult Col des Ignes.

Mont Blanc de Cheilon and the fast-receding Glacier de Cheilon

up the slope to a point where the paths split. Less than 100 metres to the right are ladders with a chain on the rock which ease the ascent to the **Pas de Chèvres** (2855m, 4hr 15min). There is a metal stairway with platforms and

The ladders are for most the easiest way to cross to the Val d'Hérens

guard rails fitted to the rockface, at the top of which a path descends on the eastern side of the ridge to join that from Col de Riedmatten. Unless you prefer boulders to ladders by a large margin, or a thunder storm is brewing, the ladders are a shorter and more straightforward route.

Alternatively, for the Col de Riedmatten fork left and climb an unrelentingly steep, boulder and scrambly slope to gain the narrow notch of **Col de Riedmatten** (2919m, 4hr 20min) and a window onto a new world. The final climb up the gully to the col can be aggravated by loose grit and requires some effort.

Trading shadows for sunshine on my first crossing of the col we gained that rocky cleft and light suddenly flooded ahead, washing a land of snow, ice, rock and a distant slope of grass. Below, the ridge fell into a basin of mountain-ejected debris, but our eyes were uninterested in any of this, for our attention was held by the crest of Pigne d'Arolla, by the great iced gateau of Mont Collon, by the sharp stiletto blade of the Matterhorn's upper reaches far off, by a vast wall of rock notable for the little spire of the Aiguille de la Tsa projecting from it, and by the snow-wrapped Dent Blanche on the far side of that wall.

From the Pas de Chèvres the path is a gentle descent, and the Col de Riedmatten path joins from the left in 15min. From the Col de Riedmatten the path is clearly defined although steep at first. It leads into an undulating bowl of grassland where it then veers to the right and joins the main path coming from the Pas de Chèvres.

Curving left to head east the path, clear and undemanding, takes you easily down towards Arolla. Mont Collon disappears from view, but Pigne d'Arolla grows in stature on the right with the long Tsijiore Nouve glacier carving its way in a deep trench behind a grass-covered wall of moraine. Then, as you approach Arolla, so Mont Collon reappears like an island in a sea of ice.

The path divides two or three times, but you simply follow the waymarked trail all the way down to **Arolla** (6hr).

PIGNE D'AROLLA AND MONT COLLON

An easy snow mountain that neighbours Mont Blanc de Cheilon to the east, the Pigne D'Arolla is often ascended by ski-mountaineers during a spring traverse of the classic Haute Route. An outstanding viewpoint, from it can be seen in one vast panorama most of the mountains of the Pennine Alps that feature on the Chamonix–Zermatt route, as well as the chain of the Bernese Alps. The Gran Paradiso and other peaks of the Graian Alps are also visible, and it has been claimed that the Mediterranean can be detected from the summit on a clear day. The first ascent was made by AW Moore, Horace Walker and their guide, the 'fearless' Jakob Anderegg, in July 1865. At 3796m, it's a distinctive peak recognised from afar.

More than any other, Mont Collon is the dominant feature of the Arolla valley (the upper south-western arm of Val d'Hérens). Despite its modest altitude (3637m), the rocky buttresses, snow domes and apparent bulk give this mountain an imposing stature out of all proportion to its true size. Glaciers flow round its east and west flanks like icy calipers, effectively giving Mont Collon the appearance of an island peak, but to the south it is attached to the higher L'Evêque by way of the Col de la Mitre. Mont Collon was first climbed by GE Foster with H Baumann and J Kronig in 1867. There are several routes of varying grades adorning its face, pillars and ridges today.

AROLLA (2006M)

This small mountaineering centre and minor ski resort was one of the first to be 'adopted' by the British. In 1921 the skeletons of a man and a chamois, along with a rifle and coins dating from before 1850, were revealed by a shrinking glacier. Attractively set among woods of larch and Arolla pine, Arolla is slowly expanding, but it remains one of the smallest villages on the Walker's Haute Route. As a base for a mountaineer's first alpine season it takes a lot of beating, while it also makes a very fine walking centre. (See *Walking in the Valais*, Kev Reynolds, published by Cicerone Press, for ideas.)

Accommodation (hotels, pension, dortoir), camping, restaurants, shops, postbus link with Les Haudères and Evolène. Further information from: Office du Tourisme, 1986 Arolla (tel 027 283 10 83, **www.arolla.com**). Lower-priced accommodation: Chalet Les Ecureuils, 28 places (tel 027 283 14 68, **www.immo. arolla.org**); Chalet Le Sporting, 47 dortoir places – below Arolla (tel 027 283 14 06); Hôtel de la Tza, beds and 64 dortoir places – 10min below Arolla (tel 027

283 14 06, www.latza.ch); Hôtel du Glacier, beds and dortoir places (tel 027 283 12 18); Hotel Kurhaus, beds and dortoir places (tel 027 283 70 00, www.hotel-kurhaus.arolla.com); Hôtel Mont Collon (027 283 11 91); Hôtel du Pigne (tel 027 283 71 00). Possible room(s) to rent – enquire at the village shop opposite the tourist office/post office. There is also pension (and dortoir) accommodation at the hamlet of La Gouille, 1hr 45min further on – see Stage 8 for details.

The most direct route to the Hôtel de la Tza is via a yellow waymarked path which begins on the right immediately before Hôtel du Glacier. In 10min this slopes easily down to the road directly opposite Hôtel de la Tza.

The long-established Bournissen Sports is the first outdoor store on the trail, so provides an opportunity to replace any kit; there will be other stores in Zinal.

Alternative route via the Cabane des Dix

From the signed junction about 45min from the **Pas du Chat**, ignore the left-hand option to Col de Riedmatten, and instead keep along the moraine rib. The path is clear and views ever interesting, and as you make progress along it you can see the deep col of Pas de Chèvres on the far side of the glacier.

Towards the end of the moraine the path veers right, descends into the ablation valley, then rises over grass slopes and onto screes by which you gain the north-west shoulder of the Tête Noir, which hides not only Mont Blanc de Cheilon, but also the Cabane des Dix.

As you rise towards the saddle on this shoulder, a wonderful panorama is seen off to the left (east). Far beyond the Monts Rouges ridge a jagged collection of peaks holds your attention. In that collection is the Matterhorn, whose profile from here is quite different to that normally seen from Zermatt. It appears as a distant stiletto with a marked shelf projecting to the south just beneath the summit. Then, when you gain the saddle, the vast pyramid of the north face of Mont Blanc de Cheilon appears before you, while the hut can be seen below, perched on top of a rocky knoll. The path winds down into a glacial plain, crosses a stream or two, then strikes directly up the slope to reach the **Cabane des Dix** (4hr). ◀

The Cabane des Dix occupies a truly spectacular site with a direct view onto the north face of Mont Blanc de Cheilon, and makes an ideal site for a lunch stop.

The Cabane des Dix

CABANE DES DIX (2928m) 150 places, restaurant service, fully staffed from mid-March to end of May, and from July to mid-September (tel 027 281 15 23, **www.cabanedesdix.ch**, advance booking essential). Owned by the Monte Rosa section of the Swiss Alpine Club, this refuge is one of the busiest in the Alps and is used by walkers, climbers and ski-tourers alike, so all intending to use it for overnight lodging are urged to telephone in advance.

Check with the hut guardian for the latest routing across the glacier, which has been moved further south in recent years. The glacier crossing does not require gear.

From Cabane des Dix descend the knoll on a clear path that winds leftwards (south) to the edge of the rubble-strewn Glacier de Cheilon, and follow the marked route across it. Marker poles, cairns and waymarks give directions. It's an easy crossing with practically no crevasses, but it is important to follow the precise line shown by the markers. ◄

On reaching the far side continuing waymarks and cairns steer you slanting left towards the base of Col de Riedmatten. As it negotiates a chaos of rocks and boulders, this section can be quite tiring. On gaining a clear path coming from Lac des Dix and leading to Col de Riedmatten, bear right, and a few paces later the path forks. The left branch climbs to Col de Riedmatten, while the right-hand path goes to the ladders of the Pas de Chèvres. This latter path tucks against the base of the ridge, and traverses beneath it with long sections of fixed chains as far as the foot of the ladders. A stairway with platforms and guard rails fitted to the rockface brings you to the **Pas de Chèvres** (2855m) in less than 2hr from the refuge.

A very fine panorama now unfolds, which includes the Veisivi–Bertol wall above Arolla, with the delicate little Aiguille de la Tsa projecting from it, and beyond that the top of Dent Blanche, summit cone of the Matterhorn, Mont Collon and many more. It's a col to relax on and enjoy, before tearing yourself away to tackle the descent to Arolla as described in the main route.

The narrow cleft of the Col de Riedmatten is a gateway to a new world

STAGE 8
Arolla – Lac Bleu – Les Haudères – La Sage

Start	Arolla (2006m)
Distance	11.5km
Total ascent	520m
Total descent	860m
Time	4hr
Low point	Les Haudères (1452m)
Accommodation	La Gouille (2hr): pension, dortoir; Les Haudères (3hr 15min): hotels, camping; La Sage: dortoir, hotel; Villa (+15min): simple rooms (self-catering only)
Transport options	Postbus (Arolla–Les Haudères–La Sage–Villa)

Although this is a short and reasonably undemanding stage, it is not really practical to go beyond La Sage (or Villa), as neither the crossing of Col du Tsaté nor Col de Torrent offers prospects of accommodation for at least another 5hr. It is nonetheless a stage to enjoy for there are numerous features to brighten the way.

The route to Les Haudères by way of Lac Bleu is designed to avoid all but the very briefest sections of road walking, in addition to providing an excuse to visit one of the best-loved sites around Arolla. There are charming views when you gaze back the way you have come; there are woodlands and small meadows, but the route to Lac Bleu has a few short exposed sections too, safeguarded with fixed chains or cables; and between Lac Bleu and La Gouille there's a small alp hamlet. From La Gouille a wooded path leads to some lovely old houses on the edge of Les Haudères, a mountaineering centre at the head of Val d'Hérens, where it forks into the tributary glens of Arolla and Ferpècle. Then, leaving Les Haudères, a steady rising traverse path ascends the hillside to La Sage.

From the village square in Arolla walk down the side road towards Hôtel du Glacier. About 40 metres before the hotel take a signed path on the left which climbs above chalets, then eases towards the red-shuttered buildings of

BOOKING AHEAD

Before setting out on this stage it is advisable to telephone ahead to book rooms for the night as there's limited accommodation in both La Sage and Villa. Failure to secure beds in either of these places will necessitate a return to Les Haudères. If this should happen it might be worth taking an early postbus next morning to La Sage (for the Col du Tsaté route) or Villa (for the Col de Torrent option).

From Arolla to Zermatt the Walker's Haute Route is shared by the Tour of the Matterhorn, most of whose trekkers will be walking towards you. But their numbers could clearly have an impact on the amount of accommodation available. For details of this route, which crosses two crevassed glaciers on its 10-day circuit, see *Tour of the Matterhorn* by Hilary Sharp (Cicerone Press).

the Centre Alpin. Go between the buildings and onto a footpath rising into woodland. ▶ On coming to a signed junction take the upper path (*Chemin difficile* – direction Louché, Lac Bleu and La Gouille); the lower branch is an easier but less interesting path which also goes to Louché and Lac Bleu.

Climbing steeply at times, the path picks a way among alpenrose and juniper, and at the upper tree level crosses a stream just below a group of alp huts. Wandering across an open slope, with lovely backward

In bad weather, you can opt to descend through meadows beside the river in the valley bottom.

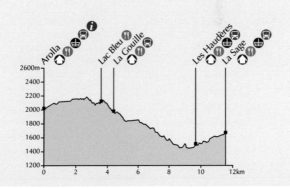

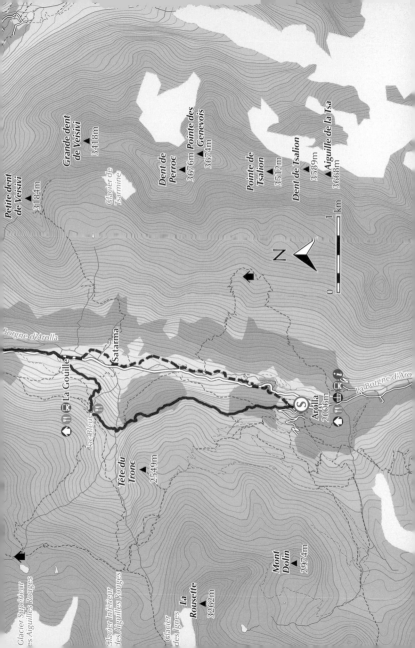

Petite dent
de Veisivi
3184m

Grande dent
de Veisivi
3418m

Glacier de
Tsarmine

Dent de
Perroc
3676m

Pointe des
Genevois
3674m

Pointe de
Tsalion
3512m

Dent de Tsalion
3589m

Aiguille de la Tsa
3668m

N

0   1   km

Borgne d'Arolla

Satarma

La Gouille

Lac Bleu

La Borgne d'Aro

S

Arolla
2006m

Tête du
Tronc
2549m

Mont
Dolin
2974m

La
Rousette
3262m

Glacier Supérieur
des Aiguilles Rouges

Glacier Inférieur
des Aiguilles Rouges

Glacier
des Ignes

views to Mont Collon and the Pigne d'Arolla, the path crosses more streams, then re-enters woodland after tackling the first of several slightly exposed sections protected either by fixed cables or chains.

The route develops into something of a switchback, an undulating trail that absorbs the natural line. After a very exposed section overlooking the hamlet of **Satarma**, cross a high point, then descend very steeply (caution when wet) to two footbridges. At the foot of the next steep descent the path forks – the lower branch being the alternative (yellow waymarked) path that offered an easier option from Arolla. Take the upper fork to cross two more streams before twisting uphill among larches. The continuing path contours, then climbs again to top a grass bluff overlooking the aptly named **Lac Bleu** (2090m, 1hr 30min). ◀

Once again there's a fine view back to Mont Collon, although Pigne d'Arolla has disappeared at this point.

Pigne d'Arolla, seen from the path to Lac Bleu

Lac Bleu

Go down to the tarn's outflow past a *buvette* and along a footpath to a tiny alp hamlet (Louché) where cheese and milk may be purchased. Just below the hamlet the path forks again. Branch right and descend a steep grass slope, then go through forest to reach the small hamlet of **La Gouille** (2hr).

> **LA GOUILLE (1845m)** Accommodation at Pension du Lac Bleu, 33 places in rooms and dortoir, meals and refreshments (tel 027 283 11 66, **www. pension-du-lac-bleu.ch**); postbus to Les Haudères.

Bear left down the Arolla–Les Haudères road for about 200 metres, then slope off to the right on a path waymarked yellow and black. This eases along the hillside below the road and soon joins a track near the tiny white-painted chapel of **St Barthélemy** (1821m). Continue down the track, and when it forks wander straight ahead. With gentle gradients the track leads

135

The old houses of Les Haudères (photo: Madeline Williams)

downvalley and eventually comes to a group of handsome old timber houses. Just beyond these join the main road, bear right and walk into **Les Haudères** (3hr 15min).

LES HAUDÈRES (1452M)

This attractive, unspoilt and typically Valaisian village is mostly contained in a triangle delineated by two roads and a steep hillside at the head of Val d'Hérens. Most of its buildings are of timber on a stone base, with granaries mingled among the houses and small garden plots. Its houses are adorned with window boxes bursting with flowers, while the granaries, or hay barns, are perched on staddle stones to deter rodents. Les Haudères makes a good base for a walking holiday, the two adjacent valleys (of Arolla and Ferpècle) being of special interest and having superb high mountain views.

Hotels, camping, restaurants, shops, PTT, postbus. For the central tourist information for the area tel 027 283 40 00, **www.valdherens.ch**. Lower-priced hotels: Des Alpes, 16 beds (tel 027 283 16 77); Les Mélèzes, 28 beds (tel 027 283 11 55); Dents de Veisivi, 18 beds (tel 027 283 11 01); Edelweiss, 35 beds (tel 027 283 11 07).

After crossing the bridge at the village entrance bear right on the road heading towards Ferpècle, La Forclaz and La Sage, but then turn left opposite Hôtel des Alpes. Wander along a narrow street lined with attractive, typically Valaisian timber buildings, and follow through on an upper village street where there are both direction signs and waymarks. ▶

This interesting stroll takes you past some of the oldest and best of Les Haudères's buildings.

From the old centre of the village by a log water fountain, a signed path takes you onto the climb to La Sage and a track continues uphill at a steady angle among trees. When it bends sharply to the right leave the track for a path continuing straight ahead. When this forks take the upper, right-hand path which leads between meadows and onto the road near La Sage.

Almost immediately take a narrow tarmac road on the left. It winds between pastures and brings you up a slope to pass Hôtel de la Sage before coming onto the road in the middle of **La Sage** (4hr).

LA SAGE (1667M)

This small village is built on a natural terrace some 250m above the valley, with charming views towards Pigne d'Arolla, or south-east to the snowfields and glaciers that spread between Dent Blanche and the Bouquetins ridge. A frequent postbus service travels between Les Haudères and the roadhead at Villa, passing through La Sage. As with several other villages in Val d'Hérens, local women may occasionally be seen wearing traditional long black dresses, decorated with colourful embroidery.

Accommodation, restaurant, shop, postbus. For the central tourist information for the area tel 027 283 40 00, **www.valdherens.ch**. 24 beds plus 7 in 'Randonneurs' apartment at Hôtel de la Sage (tel 027 283 24 20, **www.hoteldelasage.com**). 30 dortoir places at Café-Restaurant L'Ecureuil (tel 027 283 24 55).

Limited (self-catering) accommodation is available at Villa, the next village along the road, about 15min from La Sage. There is also B&B accommodation in the village on the path to Evolène (079 359 80 12, **www.balcon-herens.ch**).

OPTIONS INTO ZINAL

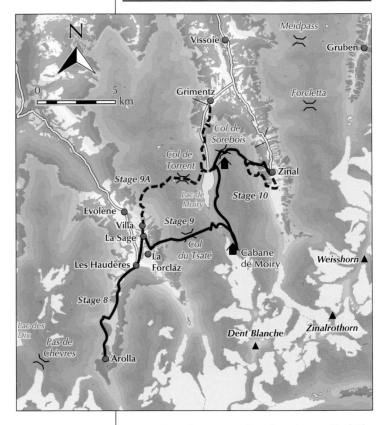

From La Sage there are two broad routings to Zinal. The higher route (Stages 9 and 10) crosses the Col du Tsaté and, after dropping to the upper Moiry valley, climbs a moraine to the Cabane de Moiry, a modern, high alpine hut for an overnight stay overlooking the Moiry glacier. The next day the route traverses high above the Lac de

Moiry before crossing the Col de Sorebois and descending to Zinal.

The alternative routing (Stages 9A and 10A) crosses the Col de Torrent to the Barrage de Moiry and the following day crosses the Col de Sorebois. This route is shorter and allows the Chamonix–Zermatt trekker to descend to Grimentz. If your plan is to take in the Hôtel Weisshorn on Stage 11, this is more direct. Unless the weather is poor, our view is that a night at the Cabane de Moiry should be a part of the trek.

STAGE 9
La Sage – Col du Tsaté – Cabane de Moiry

Start	La Sage (1667m)
Distance	15km
Total ascent	1680m
Total descent	520m
Time	6hr
High point	Col du Tsaté (2868m)
Accommodation	Cabane de Moiry: SAC refuge
Transport options	None

Between Val d'Hérens and Val d'Anniviers – the next major valley on the journey heading east – lies the small but lovely Val de Moiry, a tributary glen that feeds Anniviers. A long ridge system which maintains an altitude of 2900m and more extends north-westward from the Grand Cornier, making an effective divide between the Vals d'Hérens and Moiry, but with several accessible cols enabling walkers to cross from one to the other. Col du Tsaté is the lowest and most direct of these crossing points for anyone staying in La Sage and planning to visit Cabane de Moiry, while Col de Torrent further north (Stage 9A) will be the choice of walkers aiming for either the dortoir at the Barrage de Moiry or Grimentz.

The rocky Col du Tsaté forms a break in the ridge linking Pointe du Bandon and the Couronne de Bréona, and although early Baedeker guides spoke of it as being 'toilsome' (an accurate description), there's nothing difficult about it – a long, steep walk over grass slopes with an upper stony basin just below the col, followed by an equally steep, but much shorter, descent on the eastern side.

Cabane de Moiry stands on a rocky knoll overlooking the Moiry glacier in such a spectacular position that all effort to reach it will be considered worthwhile. The final approach to it climbs along a wall of lateral moraine, followed by a steep zig-zag path up rocks. It's quite a demanding route, but a rewarding one, and from the hut one gains an amazing head-on view of the Moiry icefall. Of all lodgings on the Chamonix–Zermatt walk, this must rank among the finest for its setting.

From the centre of **La Sage** walk down the road in the direction of Les Haudères, and about 50 metres beyond

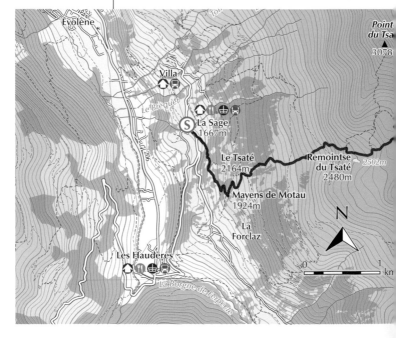

Café-Restaurant L'Ecureuil bear left onto a tarmac lane rising into forest where it becomes a track. After passing a few alp buildings come to a junction of tracks, and bear left to continue rising in larchwoods. In another 2min the track forks again. Curve right and in 25min go round a left-hand hairpin. Shortly before reaching Mayens de Motau the track bends once more and you gain a view of the Ferpècle glacier, the top of the Dent Blanche and the rocky eminence of the Pointes de Veisivi. So come to the huddle of buildings of **Mayens de Motau** (1924m, 40min, water supply), a small alp hamlet built on a steep open hillside enjoying fine views.

Above the hamlet the track stays close to a stream, narrows to a footpath which soon crosses to the left of the stream, then climbs again quite steeply alongside more larchwoods. After about 1hr 10min come to another

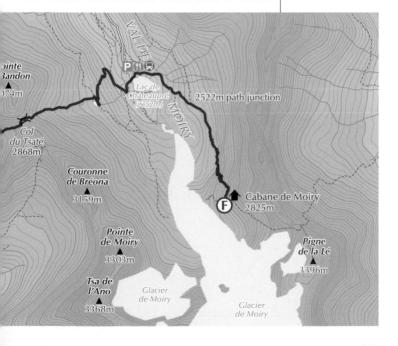

group of alp buildings, **Le Tsaté** (2164m). Keeping left of these buildings continue uphill to cross a farm track, and climb on up the steep hillside on a narrow path which leads to a solitary hut just below another section of unmade farm road (1hr 30min).

Veer left and slant up to the road, then cross to a continuing path which now climbs with more generous loops to gain height, before swinging to the right (south-east) and arriving at **Remointse du Tsaté** (2480m, 2hr) – two long cowsheds and a small dairyman's hut. These buildings are situated at the entrance to a grass basin in which there's a small tarn, unseen from here. Immediately beyond the cowsheds turn right on a track, and a few paces later veer left (red–white waymarks) on a faint path across a little meadow. Cross a stream, then walk up to a lovely flowery meadow in which you can see the small unnamed tarn to your right (2502m).

Keep well to the left of the tarn and follow the path as it rises into a second basin where the way forks. Keep with the right-hand option, rising to a crucifix at the entrance to a third and final basin – this one much more austere and stony than the previous two, at the head of which is Col du Tsaté.

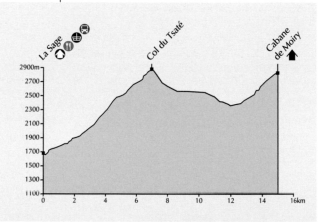

Passing just to the right of the crucifix the path crosses the stony bed of the valley, then rises on the left-hand walling hillside. As height is gained the way grows progressively more rocky until at last you emerge onto the summit of **Col du Tsaté** (2868m, 3hr 30min).

Looking back from the Col du Tsaté (photo: Madeline Williams)

VAL DE MOIRY

The small glen of Val de Moiry feeds into the longer Val d'Anniviers, of which it forms the south-western tributary. It rises in a wedge of peaks whose nodal point is the Grand Cornier (3962m), and in whose upper ridges a basin of névé gives birth to the Moiry glacier. Below the glacier two small tarns are used as settlement reservoirs to reduce the flow of glacial silt into the larger dammed Lac de Moiry below. Along the hillsides east and west of the lake a very fine path has been created more or less following the 2500m contour, and is promoted as the Haut Tour du Lac, from which the full extent of the valley is on display (a 5hr circuit). Below the Barrage de Moiry the glen is green and wooded towards Grimentz, an attractive village near the valley mouth and the only one in Val de Moiry. In summer a frequent postbus service runs between Grimentz and Parking du Glacier. At the barrage there's a restaurant, with a dortoir on the hillside above the east side of the dam.

Climbing the moraine to the Cabane de Moiry (photo: Madeline Williams)

The east side of the ridge which falls to the Val de Moiry is also stony at first, and the descent steep in places as it crosses screes and slopes of shale before coming onto a pleasant grass shelf (about 20min below the col), from which you gain a first view of the Moiry icefall and refuge – the latter stands atop rock slabs to the left of the icefall. Continue down to a small tarn and a path junction at 2547m.

MOIRY GLACIER ICEFALL

The icefall of the Moiry glacier is among the most impressive of its kind in the Pennine Alps, and that the mountain walker can gaze upon it from so close and safe a vantage point as the hut makes it extra special. In *The Alps in 1864*, the Victorian pioneer AW Moore wrote about it in glowing terms, referring to it as: 'a tremendous ice-fall of great height and very steep. The lower part … extends completely from one side of the glacier to the other, but higher up, under the Pigne de la Lex, is a belt of smooth ice, which we had no doubt would give access to the field of névé above the fall. Below this great cascade of séracs, the ice is as compact and level as above it is steep and dislocated. Indeed, I never saw an ice-fall confined within such plainly defined limits, or terminate so abruptly.'

In order to continue to the cabane on the most direct route go right, then take a left branch about a minute later, signed to Lac du Glacier. It descends in zig-zags, now with the dammed Lac de Moiry seen to the north, and eventually brings you to a track which swings down to the roadhead **Parking du Glacier** (2409m, 4hr 30min) which has a small *buvette* (refreshment hut) and a bus stop for Grimentz and Zinal.

> The **Haut Tour du Lac/Chemin 2500m** makes a traverse left and joins the route of Stage 9A at a farm, Alpage de Torrent. Should you have changed your mind about going to the Moiry refuge, you could follow this path to the farm, then descend to the Barrage de Moiry for overnight in the dortoir.

Pass to the left of the *buvette* onto a track signed to Cabane de Moiry. The track soon becomes a footpath which rises onto the east side lateral moraine walling the Moiry glacier. After picking a way along the narrow moraine crest, around 40min from the *buvette*, the path

The Moiry icefall dominates the view at the Cabane de Moiry (photo: Madeline Williams)

slopes down into the little ablation valley before climbing in zig-zags, with two small sections with cables, up rocky slopes which lead directly to the **Cabane de Moiry** (6hr).

CABANE DE MOIRY (2825m) 100 places, fully staffed with meals provision from the end of June to end of September (tel 027 475 45 34 on the day, advance booking only through the website **www. cabane-de-moiry.ch**).

CABANE DE MOIRY

Owned by the Montreux section of the Swiss Alpine Club, the Cabane de Moiry is built in a dramatic location among a horseshoe of peaks and glaciers. In 2010 the hut was extended with excellent new accommodation facilities and a magnificent glass-walled dining room overlooking the glacier. Above it to the east runs the wall of the Aiguilles de la Lé; opposite rise Couronne de Bréona, Pointe de Moiry and Tsa de l'Ano. Between the Couronne and Pointe de Moiry lies the Col de Couronne, by which access to the glen may be achieved from the head of Val d'Hérens (a more

Cabane de Moiry, an atmospheric place in which to spend a night

strenuous and less well-marked route than either Col du Tsaté or Col de Torrent), while south-east of the hut, between the last of the Aiguilles de la Lé and Pigne de la Lé, Col du Pigne offers another way over to Zinal. (Not for inexperienced mountain walkers, though.)

The hut is popular among ski-mountaineers, for several of the summits that enclose the glacier provide enjoyable ski ascents. Pigne de la Lé and Pointe de Bricola (north-west of Grand Cornier) are among the most popular, while summer ascents are made directly from the hut to Grand Cornier and all the neighbouring peaks. By virtue of its short approach from the roadhead (1hr 30min), Cabane de Moiry receives plenty of day-visitors.

STAGE 9A

La Sage – Col de Torrent –
Barrage de Moiry/Grimentz

Start	La Sage (1667m)
Distance	13km (18km to Grimentz)
Total ascent	1250m
Total descent	670m (or 1350m to Grimentz)
Time	5hr (7hr to Grimentz)
High point	Col de Torrent (2916m)
Accommodation	Villa (15min): self-catering rooms; Chalet du Barrage: dortoir; Grimentz: hotels
Transport options	Postbus (Barrage de Moiry–Grimentz)

A little over 4km north-west of Col du Tsaté (crossed on Stage 9) the higher Col de Torrent is a popular and much used link between the Vals d'Hérens and Moiry. Pastureland rises almost all the way to the col on both sides of the ridge, and views are consistently fine. The way up to the pass is a delight, while the panorama on the eastern side is the equal of anything seen so far, with the descent to the dammed Lac de Moiry being both undemanding and visually rewarding.

The dortoir above the barrage is ideally placed for the crossing of Col de Sorebois to Zinal next day, but some commercial trekking parties (and a few individuals) choose not to stay at the Chalet du Barrage, continuing instead down to Grimentz where there's a range of accommodation on offer. With this option the onward route misses Zinal completely by going directly to Hôtel Weisshorn, thereby reducing the length of the walk by one day. Details of this option are given below.

Walk up the road from La Sage to **Villa** (1714m, 15min, accommodation, refreshments, postbus to/from Les Haudères). Just across the bridge in Villa turn right opposite a small white chapel where a sign indicates the way to Mayens de Cotter, Col de Torrent, etc. Go alongside a granary, then turn right on a cobbled track that rises

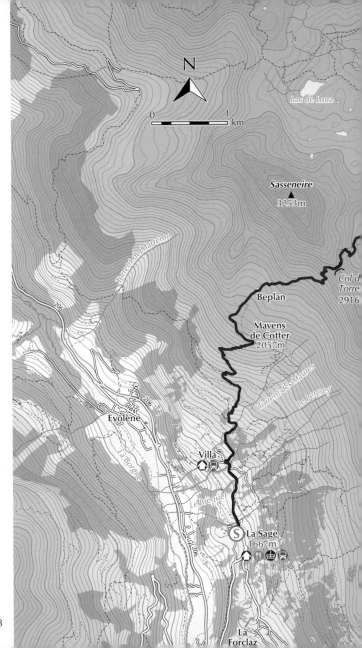

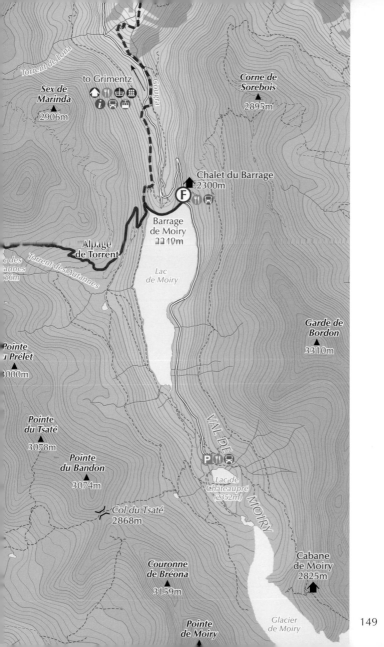

Torrent de Lona

Sex de Marinda
2906m

to Grimentz

Corne de Sorebois
2895m

Chalet du Barrage
2300m

F

Barrage de Moiry
2249m

Alpage de Torrent

Torrent des Autannes

e des annes
86m

Lac de Moiry

Pointe a Prélet
3000m

Garde de Bordon
3310m

Pointe du Tsaté
3078m

Pointe du Bandon
3074m

VAL DE MOIRY

P

Lac de Châteaupré
(2352m)

Col du Tsaté
2868m

Couronne de Bréona
3159m

Cabane de Moiry
2825m

Glacier de Moiry

Pointe de Moiry

The Dents de Vesivi and the Pigne d'Arolla from above La Sage

above the village. When the cobbles end, the track continues.

In 40min the track forks by a stream. Keep ahead to the right side of this stream and 4min later, when it makes a right-hand hairpin, leave the track to follow a path straight ahead, still along the right-hand side of the stream. The path then crosses the stream and angles up the hillside, and – climbing steadily – it then goes through a strip of larchwood and on to a footbridge and a junction of tracks. Walk ahead along a farm road, soon passing a few timber chalets, barns and a water supply.

> From the outset views are very fine, not just to those peaks behind that have grown familiar from walking beside them during the past few days, but ahead too, to mountains of the Bernese Alps on the far side of the Rhône valley. Les Diablerets and the Wildhorn massif look especially appealing.

In 1hr 10min turn a right-hand hairpin and continue to the group of farms and chalets of **Mayens de Cotter** (2057m) reached 5min later, from which views show the

Dent Blanche, Tête Blanche, Pigne d'Arolla and many other peaks. Immediately after passing a large farm building and a water trough, take a footpath cutting back to the left and rising across the steep grass hillside in long loops. ▶

This hillside is used by paragliding enthusiasts, as evidenced by a number of windsocks.

The path brings you up to and past an upstanding pillar of rock, and beyond this curves to the right onto a grass rib that leads through a basin of pastureland in which there are a few semi-derelict huts (**Beplan**). In about 2hr 30min pass a little pond on your left (2536m) and a large cairn on your right. This is a splendid vantage point with an extensive view.

Beyond the pond the path continues to rise, making a long sweep to the east before cutting back to the left in order to make the final ascent to the **Col de Torrent** (2916m, 3hr 30min). There's a large wooden cross just to the right of the actual pass, and tremendous views. To south and west the panorama includes the Mont Miné, Tête Blanche, Grande Dent de Veisivi, Mont Brulé, Pigne d'Arolla, Mont Blanc de Cheilon, Grand Combin, the Aiguilles Rouges, Rosablanche and, far off, the snowy mass of Mont Blanc. Turning to the east across the lovely Lac des Autannes and jade-green Lac de Moiry, which lie

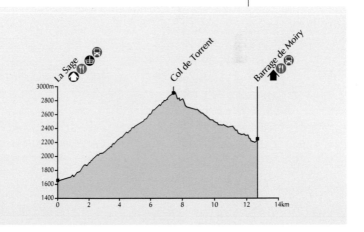

151

in the deep trough of Val de Moiry, stand the Weisshorn, Schalihorn and Pointe Sud de Moming.

For an even **broader panorama** than that won from the col, go left up the ridge for 45min (allow 1hr 30min for the round-trip) to the summit of Sasseneire (3254m), where far to the north you can just make out the line of the Jura through the Col de Cheville, while to the south the Dent Blanche, which is not seen from the Col de Torrent, dominates the view.

The Moiry glacier and its peaks with the Dent Blanche are just part of the attraction of the Lac des Autannes

A clear path descends on the Moiry side, first heading north, then swinging eastward down to undulating pastures. As you draw level with the picturesque **Lac des Autannes**, some 230m and 15min or so below the col, exquisite views are to be had across the tarn to a turmoil

of glaciers and peaks that block the head of Val de Moiry. Up there, the Pigne de la Lé, Grand Cornier and Dent Blanche cast ridges, snowfields and long streamers of ice, creating those contrasts of light and shade, height and depth, and barren upland against a foreground of soft pasture that make wandering in the Alps such a memorable experience.

Beyond the lake a good path descends rough pastures and brings you to a junction of tracks by the **Alpage de Torrent** (2481m, 4hr 15min, water supply). The route of the Haut Tour du Lac breaks off to the right, but the way to the barrage continues ahead. Remain on this track all the way to the massive **Barrage de Moiry** (2249m) at the northern end of **Lac de Moiry**. Cross the dam to a restaurant on the eastern side (5hr, refreshments, toilet, public telephone, postbus to Grimentz and Zinal). For dortoir accommodation apply at the restaurant, then take the path which climbs the slope above the parking area to reach the **Chalet du Barrage** (5hr).

> **CHALET DU BARRAGE (2300m)** Also known as the Gîte de Moiry, it has 24 dortoir places, self-catering facilities, but meals at the restaurant, open June to end of September (tel 027 475 15 48, www.moiryresto.ch).

Continuation to Grimentz

Should your plan be to visit Grimentz for overnight accommodation, recross to the western side of the barrage then take a signed footpath (a minor track) winding downhill with footpath shortcuts. In 20min one of the shortcuts brings you to a sign giving 1hr 30min to Grimentz. From here the path contours along the hillside among alpenrose, juniper and alder scrub; later with some rock-hopping. In 40min come to another junction and descend steeply to the road. Cross to the continuing path through rough pasture, then wander downstream along either bank of the stream.

The right-bank footpath eventually recrosses the stream and comes onto the road again. Walk ahead a short distance to a bus stop, where you rejoin the path which slopes below the road and shortly gives a good view down to Grimentz and the lower valley. The way loops downhill, crosses to the right side of the stream and follows a track which soon enters forest. In 1hr 30min at a junction, cross the stream once more onto a tarmac road (camping on the left), and wander down to **Grimentz** (7hr).

> **GRIMENTZ (1555m)** Accommodation, refreshments, shops, bank, PTT, postbus (to Zinal, St Luc, Vissoie, Sierre, etc). Anniviers Tourisme – Bureau de Grimentz, 3961 Grimentz (tel 027 476 1700, **www. grimentz.ch**). Lower-priced hotels: Le Mélèze, 20 beds (tel 027 475 12 87, **www.hotel-meleze.ch**); Hôtel de Moiry, 34 beds (tel 027 475 11 44, **www. hotel-grimentz.ch**).

ONWARD ROUTES FROM GRIMENTZ

- Take the **postbus** back to the Barrage de Moiry and follow **Stage 10A** to Zinal.

- Follow the **waymarked route** from Grimentz to **Zinal** (2hr 30min) where you rejoin the main Chamonix to Zermatt walk at the start of Stage 11.

- Take a **signed route** on footpaths and tracks to **Mission** (30 min) and then steeply uphill to **Hôtel Weisshorn** (described at the end of Stage 11A) in about 4hr from Grimentz.

- Take the **postbus to St-Luc**, then ride the Tignousa funicular to its top station, and walk to **Hôtel Weisshorn** in 1hr or **Cabane Bella Tola** in 30min (see Stage 11A). This could allow a crossing of the Meidpass the same day.

STAGE 10
Cabane de Moiry – Col de Sorebois – Zinal

Start	Cabane de Moiry (2825m)
Distance	19.5km
Total ascent	650m
Total descent	1800m
Time	7hr
High point	Col de Sorebois (2836m)
Accommodation	Cabane de Sorebois (4hr 50min): dortoir; Zinal: hotels, dortoir, camping
Transport options	Postbus (Barrage de Moiry–Grimentz–Zinal); cablecar (Col de Sorebois–Grimentz); cablecar (Sorebois–Zinal)

This stage, leading from the arctic splendour of the upper Val de Moiry to the deep forested trench of Val de Zinal (the upper reaches of Val d'Anniviers), entails the crossing of yet another high ridge. This time, however, the effort required to reach it is not unduly fatiguing, while the panorama that greets you on arrival at Col de Sorebois is truly memorable, with Weisshorn and Zinalrothorn on show almost all the way down to Zinal.

After descending along the moraine wall below Cabane de Moiry, a superb belvedere trail carries the route along the hillside heading north about 300m above Lac de Moiry. The hillside is noted for its alpine flowers, and there's also a good chance of catching sight of chamois or even ibex. When the contouring path meets a track above the barrage, our route breaks off to the right and climbs steeply to Col de Sorebois. The direct descent into Zinal across grass and through forest is very steep. There is an easier descent by the track – recommended for tired knees.

Descend from the hut on the same path used for the approach, and after about 50min and 1.8km, when you've left the moraine bank and the path becomes wider and easier at an altitude of about **2522m**, a path breaks to the right signed to Barrage de Moiry. This path, which forms part of the Haut Tour du Lac, follows a fairly regular

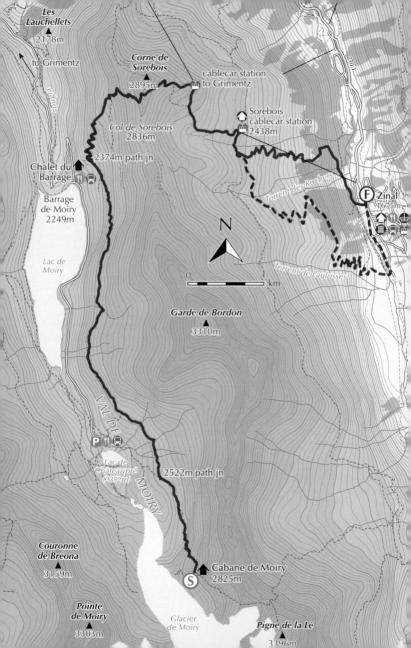

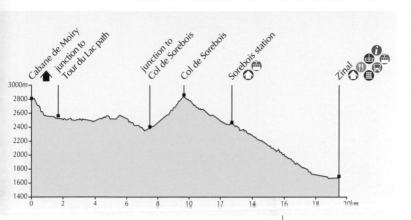

contour across the grassy hillside. After about 15min come to a junction where the left-hand option descends to the roadhead car park; the way to Col de Sorebois continues ahead.

It's a very fine undulating path offering splendid views of the glacial landscape you've left behind, and

The moraine descent from the hut has great walking but steep sides (photo: Madeline Williams)

157

Rapidly deteriorating conditions at the Col de Sorebois

Views are mostly downvalley towards Grimentz, and there's a possibility of catching sight of chamois and marmots on the way to the pass.

soon overlooks the jade-green waters of **Lac de Moiry** and the valley falling away in the distance. Towards the end of the lake the path slopes downhill to meet a grass track at 2374m (2hr 30min). Bear right (the lower route descends to the Barrage de Moiry), and begin rising in long loops. When the track begins a long sweep to the right, a red–white waymark directs you left onto a narrow path heading up the grass slope. This steep path, relaid but hardly improved in 2018, takes you all the way to the col. ◄

Come onto the saddle of **Col de Sorebois** (2836m, 4hr) to be greeted by an incredible panorama of high peaks opposite, dominated by the Weisshorn. Ignore if you can the reshaped ski terrain below and enjoy one of the finest views so far. Hard to believe, it's a view that improves as you descend.

For the descent into Val de Zinal, take a path directly ahead which contours briefly then angles slightly downhill to join a broader grass path/track beneath a chairlift and continues onto a waymarked piste (5min from the col). Pass the top of the cablecar to Grimentz. Looking

THE WEISSHORN

A beautiful mountain with three faces and three ridges, at 4506m the Weisshorn ranks as one of the highest in the Pennine Alps (the second highest standing solely in Switzerland). Forming part of that great ridge which separates Val de Zinal from the Mattertal, the Weisshorn is eye-catching from many different angles, and by the time you reach Zermatt you will have grown very familiar with it. As a mountaineer's mountain the main interest lies in its ridges, and it was by way of the East Ridge that it received its first ascent on 19 August 1861 by the pioneering Victorian scientist and mountaineer John Tyndall (1820–93), with JJ Bennen and Ulrich Wenger as his guides.

out for reroutings in this area from ski development, follow the path as it winds down the scarred hillside to the cablecar station of **Sorebois** (4hr 50min).

> **SOREBOIS (2438m)** 30 dortoir places, open mid-June to end of September (tel 027 475 20 65), refreshments, cablecar to Zinal.

VAL DE ZINAL

The name given to the upper reaches of Val d'Anniviers, Val de Zinal holds much of interest to both walkers and climbers. Indeed, some of the most varied and scenically spectacular walks of the whole Pennine Alps chain are to be enjoyed here, while the big peaks that wall it hold some dramatic routes. The head of the valley is a spectacular amphitheatre of ice and snow with Ober Gabelhorn, Mont Durand, Pointe de Zinal, Dent Blanche, Grand Cornier and the Bouquetins rising from it. Zinalrothorn, Pointe Sud de Moming, Schalihorn and Weisshorn create another cirque in the south-east, while opposite this the pasture bowl of La Lé is backed by another rocky crescent. Evidence of past glaciations can be read quite clearly within the valley itself. For a selection of walks in and around the valley, see *Walking in the Valais*, Kev Reynolds, published by Cicerone Press.

Bear right along a track for 3min, then take a footpath branching left signed to Mottec and Zinal. As it winds down the hillside it passes beneath a chairlift and

An alternative descent on a signed track that passes through La Latta takes a similar time and is easier on the knees.

the cableway, then forks. Take the right branch and soon enter forest where the path becomes much steeper and seemingly endless – a knee-jarring descent. ◄ The path is clear and obvious, and a few minutes before reaching the foot of the slope a handrail, followed by a wooden walkway and a footbridge, takes you across a stream flowing down a gully. Keep ahead at a junction 3min later. There's another footbridge to cross before you come to the Navisence and over this walk up into **Zinal** (7hr).

ZINAL (1675M)

This long-time mountaineering centre is steadily growing at its northern end. The original village, crowded with timber houses and granaries, forms an attractive line along the true right bank of the valley. Zinal is the final settlement in the long Val d'Anniviers; beyond it the valley grows increasingly wild and austere with glaciers, moraine

Morning in Zinal

banks and a glorious array of high mountains. Although the majority of walks here entail some pretty steep ascents and descents, Zinal makes an excellent base for a walking or climbing holiday.

Accommodation, camping, ATM, restaurants, shops, supermarkets, PTT, postbus (Zinal–Vissoie–St-Luc–Sierre), Bureau des Guides. Office du Tourisme: 3961 Zinal (tel 027 476 17 05, **www.zinal.ch**). Lower-priced accommodation: Hôtel Le Trift, 34 beds (tel 027 475 14 66, **www.letriftzinal.ch**); Auberge Alpina, dortoir and rooms, open mid-June to mid-October (tel 027 475 12 24, **www.auberge-alpina.ch**); Hôtel Europe (027 475 44 04, **www.europezinal.ch**); Pension de la Poste, 18 beds (tel 027 475 11 87, **http://lapostezinal.ch**). Note The proprietor at Auberge Alpina also has a chalet for rent suitable for 2–4 people, with kitchen facilities. Telephone number as above.

STAGE 10A

Barrage de Moiry – Col de Sorebois – Zinal

Start	Barrage de Moiry (2249m)
Distance	9km
Total ascent	600m
Total descent	1170m
Time	4hr
High point	Col de Sorebois (2836m)
Accommodation	Cabane de Sorebois (2hr 30min): dortoir; Zinal: hotels, dortoir, camping
Transport options	Postbus (Barrage de Moiry–Grimentz–Zinal); cablecar (Sorebois–Zinal)
Alternative route	Barrage de Moiry to Zinal or Hôtel Weisshorn via Grimentz: see details at end of Stage 9A

An easy and straightforward crossing of Col de Sorebois takes the C–Z trekker into the lovely Val de Zinal among the highest mountains of the route since leaving the Mont Blanc massif. On the ascent to the pass there's a distinct possibility of seeing chamois and marmots, while the view from the col itself is awe-inspiring.

From the dortoir just above the Barrage de Moiry wander up the track to the junction with the route of the Haut Tour du Lac which forks right. Ignore this option and continue uphill in long loops for another 20min, when your track makes a long sweep to the right. Now leave the track for a narrow red–white waymarked path rising steeply up the grass slope on the left. This leads eventually to Col de Sorebois, on occasion with steep zig-zags and long views downvalley towards Grimentz.

You should gain the easy saddle of **Col de Sorebois** (2836m) after about 1hr 45min to enjoy a magnificent panorama of high peaks dominated by the Weisshorn, that hopefully greets you on arrival.

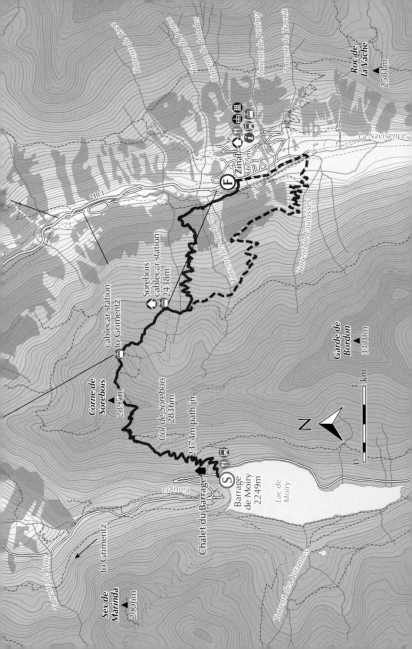

For the descent to Zinal, which passes the **Sorebois** cablecar station (2438m, 2hr 30min, accommodation, refreshments, cablecar to Zinal), please see Stage 10. Zinal (1675m) is reached in 4hr by the steep descent or 4hr 45min by the easier track descent.

Lac de Moiry

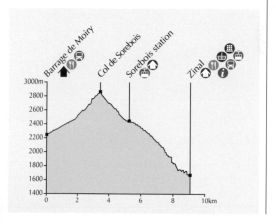

163

OPTIONS BETWEEN ZINAL AND GRUBEN

The choice is between a direct one-day crossing of the Forcletta to Gruben (Stage 11) or a two-day crossing of the Meidpass (Stages 11A and 11B). The first night of this alternative would be spent at Hôtel Weisshorn or Cabane Bella Tola – both of which have fine mountain views to north and south respectively but otherwise represent a total contrast – before the pass is crossed the next day. Both days are short at around 4hr walking time, but combined would make a long day. The Meidpass and Forcletta cols are both similarly straightforward under good conditions, so the choice of route is probably driven mostly by whether you plan to take in the oldworldly charms of the Hôtel Weisshorn, or perhaps prefer to take two easier days before the Augstbordpass and Europaweg days to come.

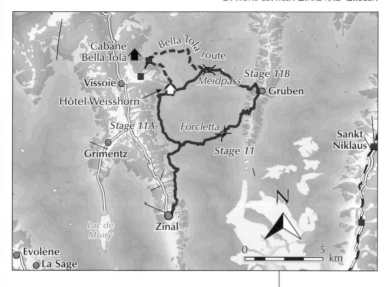

The upper part of the Forcletta on the descent to Gruben

STAGE 11
Zinal – Forcletta – Gruben

Start	Zinal (1675m)
Distance	17km
Total ascent	1250m
Total descent	1100m
Time	6hr
High point	Forcletta (2874m)
Accommodation	Gruben: hotel (beds, matratzenlager/dortoir and chalets)
Transport options	None

The next valley on the eastbound route is the little-known Turtmanntal, with Gruben (otherwise known as Meiden) being the first German-speaking community of the walk. It's a lovely half-forgotten backwater, for the valley is occupied only in summer. Not long after the cattle have been taken down to farms in lowland Switzerland, Gruben closes up until the following spring.

There are two main ways of reaching the Turtmanntal from Zinal: via the Forcletta as per this stage, and over the Meidpass via Hôtel Weisshorn or Cabane Bella Tola as described under Stages 11A and 11B. Both are fine crossings, but the Forcletta has the edge as it is the more direct and, for walkers with limited time available, makes the trek to Zermatt one day shorter than the Meidpass option. It is a magnificent crossing, despite missing the opportunity of staying overnight in Hôtel Weisshorn – a memorable experience and, to many, a highlight of the Walker's Haute Route.

The waymarked Rt 6 starts at a junction at the north end of Zinal, but the waymarks are then missing.

Begin in the centre of Zinal, and walk up a narrow road between Hôtel Le Trift and the village church. ◄ After passing between apartment blocks, branch left towards an extensive block of apartments. About 3min from the church arrive at a road opposite a major group of apartments where a signpost directs you up a service road (Les Liddes) – direction Barneuza Alpage and Hôtel Weisshorn. This takes you between buildings, then you veer left towards a parking area, then right on a rising

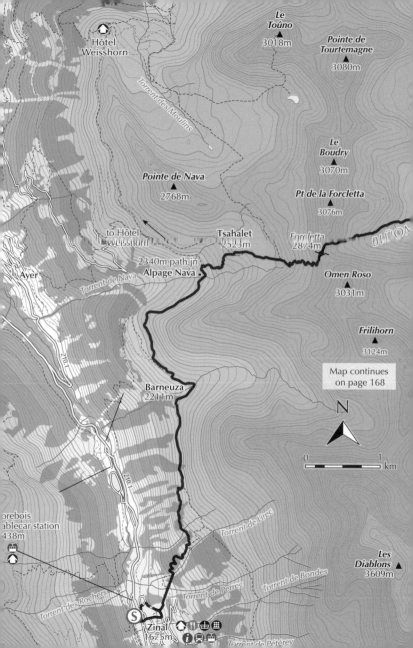

Hôtel
Weisshorn

Le Toûno
3018m

Pointe de Tourtemagne
3080m

Le Boudry
3070m

Pointe de Nava
2768m

Pt de la Forcletta
3076m

Tsahalet
2523m

Forcletta
2874m

BLÜON

to Hôtel
Weisshorn

2340m path jn
Alpage Nava

Omen Roso
3031m

Ayer

Torrent de Nava

Frilihorn
3124m

Barneuza
2211m

Map continues
on page 168

N

0   1
|___|___|___|___|___| km

orebois
ablecar station
438m

Torrent de Lirec

Les Diablons
3609m

Torrent de Perrec

Torrent de Bondes

S

Torrent des Rochers

Zinal
675m

Torrent de Pétérey

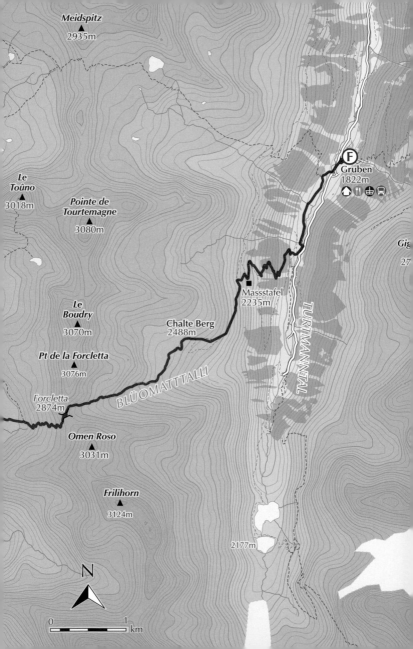

gravel track among larch trees. Go through a tunnel and cross an avalanche defence system.

Once across this the path, which is broad and well-trodden, begins to make height, but then forks about 15min from the start. Take the left branch, cross a stream, then climb by a series of steep zig-zags that take you high above the valley. After about 40min go through a gate, and shortly after take a right fork to rise across an open grass slope, at the top of which the path forks by a low building signed to Lirec. Turn sharply left and climb again into forest where the gradient eases to a more gently rising traverse, and 1hr from the start you come out of the trees to a minor path junction. Continue ahead over a brief hillside shelf (2173m) with a charming backward view to Pigne de la Lé, Grand Cornier and Dent Blanche, while ahead you gaze across the Rhône valley to the line of the Bernese Alps.

Coming out of woodland, the path now develops into a superb belvedere heading north along the hillside, and in due course you will come to the isolated farm of **Barneuza Alpage** (2211m, 1hr 45min). Immediately beyond the alp buildings there's a junction of paths; the trail to take is marked to Hôtel Weisshorn – the upper path rising ahead.

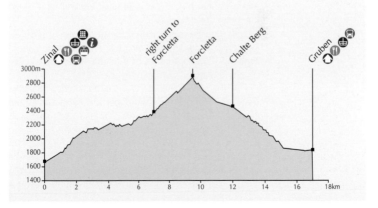

The Augstbordpass crossed on Stage 12 (the middle of the three valleys) comes into view at the Forcletta

About 5min beyond Barneuza cross a rock tip. Eventually turn a spur and cut into a deep combe whose hillsides are carpeted with juniper, bilberry and alpenrose, and you gain a view ahead towards the Forcletta. Immediately after crossing a stream come to the solitary hut of **Alpage Nava** (2340m, 2hr 20min). A few paces beyond this there's another signed junction. Take the path which climbs to the right (direction Forcletta and Gruben). It rises over grass slopes drained by a stream and is faint in places, but with sufficient red–white waymarks to direct the way.

Skirting the right-hand slope of a bowl of pastureland enter an upper level, bear left, then rise to the alp of **Tsahalet** (2523m) marked by a large wooden cross. This is gained about 20min from Alpage Nava.

At the right-hand end of the cattle sheds waymarks direct the continuing path across a rucked and pitted grassland, on the far side of which a clear path takes you up rocky slopes. The way climbs easily in long zig-zags to gain the **Forcletta** (2874m, 3hr 45min), a bare saddle in a ridge stubbed with individual peaklets. Ahead lies the glen of **Blüomatttalli**, which appears stony and barren – although as you descend through it, you will discover it is full of alpine plants. ◄

Looking back from the pass, distant views include the Aiguilles Rouges above Arolla.

170

Slant left across a slope of shale, then ease down the left-hand side of the shallow Blüomatttalli where a stream drains between great cushions of moss and flowering plants. Towards the lower end of the glen the Brunegghorn comes into view to the right across the Turtmanntal, then its long glacier with the Bishorn looking huge to the right of that, and the graceful north ridge of the Weisshorn rising above the Bishorn.

'I doubt whether there is a more spiky panorama to be seen in the Alps than this view across the Turtmanntal from the Forcletta descent,' wrote Showell Styles in *Backpacking in the Alps and Pyrenees*.

THE TURTMANNTAL

The Turtmanntal is one of the shortest valleys in the Pennine Alps, and one of the least developed. Access from the Rhône valley is by a steeply twisting road via Oberems, but unusually for Switzerland there is no postbus service above that village, although there are privately run summer bus services. The valley itself rises in the south, where the combined ridges of Brunegghorn, Bishorn and Tête de Milon form a lofty wall that never drops below 3500m. (The Weisshorn rises above and to the south of Bishorn and Tête de Milon.) Both the Turtmann and Brunegg glaciers sweep down from this wall and weld together beneath Les Diablons. Below this junction, on the right bank of the glacier, stands the Turtmann Hut (2520m, 74 places, 3hr from Gruben), base for climbs on such peaks as the Tête de Milon, Bishorn, Brunegghorn and Barrhorn, the last of these having a tremendous view of the Mattertal and the Mischabel peaks opposite. The valley is completely pastoral, with a number of farms and small hamlets. Cattle graze the lower pastures; sheep roam higher on the hillsides.

Yet again the graceful Weisshorn announces its looming presence. In his classic book *The Playground of Europe* Leslie Stephen wrote of the view from just outside Gruben: 'Above us rose the Weisshorn in one of the most sublime aspects of that almost faultless mountain. The Turtmann glacier, broad and white with deep regular crevasses, formed a noble approach, like the staircase of some superb palace. Above this rose the huge mass of the mountain, firm and solid as though its architect wished to eclipse the

The upper Turtmann valley and the glaciated Bishorn

Pyramids. And, higher still, its lofty crest, jagged and apparently swaying from side to side, seemed to be tossed into the blue atmosphere far above the reach of mortal man. Nowhere have I seen a more delicate combination of mountain massiveness, with soaring and delicately carved pinnacles pushed to the verge of extravagence. Yet few people know of this side of a peak, which every one has admired from the Riffel [above Zermatt].'

Views of the Bishorn, Weisshorn and the snow crest leading to the Tête de Milon are tremendous from here.

The path now veers left over rolling pastures and slopes down to the farm buildings of **Chalte Berg** (2488m, 4hr 20min). ◄

Pass between the alp buildings, where the route is guided by waymarks, directly down the grass slope beyond the alp to an unmade farm road. Turn left along it, and after about 150 metres bear right on a footpath which descends a little, then runs parallel to the road, later dropping well below it to more alp huts at **Massstafel** (2235m). When the path brings you onto the road once more, turn right along it for a short distance, then find the continuing path on the right, directly opposite the last hut. This soon brings you onto the road yet again.

There are two routes down to Gruben:

- starting at a hairpin bend just above where you come onto the road, this option makes a **long traverse** across the hillside to Mittel Stafel where it joins the route from Meidpass (Stage 11B) to descend to Gruben. On this route watch out for the path signing. If you miss it, a long struggle in a wood lies ahead;

- the **shorter, recommended option** described here crosses the road and turns right to descend below it directly into the valley.

Cross the road onto the path, which descends below it and soon enters forest where the way zig zags down. At times the undergrowth beside the path crowds the way, although there's nothing difficult about the descent. This finally brings you to the valley bed by more farm buildings about 1km above Gruben.

Walk towards the valley road, but do not cross the Turtmänna river. Instead take a faint grass path on the left bank and follow this downstream towards the village. ▶ In 15min come to a path junction near two chalets. Turn right, cross the river and enter **Gruben** (6hr).

Forestry operations in this area may cause a small detour.

GRUBEN (1822M)

Also known as Meiden, this small village ('more like a Swiss village of the Golden Age of Mountaineering than any other' according to Showell Styles) is the only one in the valley proper – Oberems and Unterems are at the entrance. It consists of a neat cluster of chalets, trim white chapel and hotel above flood-level on the right bank of the Turtmänna stream, idyllically placed between the Meidpass and Augstbordpass by which you leave the valley on the Walker's Haute Route. The Hotel Schwarzhorn is by far the largest building in the valley with rooms and matratzenlager/dortoir accommodation. The Restaurant Waldesruh, 5min down-valley is no longer operating. New accommodation in the Grindjisand Mountain Inn (23 beds and dortoirs, www.mountaininn.ch) is currently booked through the Hotel Schwarzhorn. German is the main language spoken from here on.

Accommodation, refreshments, shop, bus. Hotel Schwarzhorn, beds and matratzen-lager, open June to October (tel 027 932 1414, **www.hotelschwarzhorn.ch**).

STAGE 11A
Zinal – Hôtel Weisshorn/Cabane Bella Tola

Start	Zinal (1675m)
Distance	11km (16km to Cabane Bella Tola)
Total ascent	810m (or 1000m)
Total descent	150m (or 330m)
Time	3hr 30min (or 5–5hr 30min)
High point	2400m
Accommodation	Hôtel Weisshorn; Cabane Bella Tola: mountain refuge
Transport options	Postbus (Zinal to St-Luc), then funicular to Tignousa

The path which runs along a hillside shelf high on the east wall of Val d'Anniviers between Zinal and Hôtel Weisshorn provides one of the great walks of Switzerland, and presents such stunning views to the head of the valley that you will probably wish it were possible to walk backwards! The magic of the upper Val d'Anniviers (Val de Zinal), with its crowded mass of snow and ice giants, makes this an alpine wonderland. As you will want to absorb as much of that magic as possible, the day's walk will inevitably take a lot longer than the basic times quoted above.

As for Hôtel Weisshorn, this large Victorian building lost some of its former eccentricity when it was refurbished a few years ago, but the charm remains, as does the surprise of its setting. A night spent there, although expensive, is counted among the highlights of the Chamonix to Zermatt walk by a large number of trekkers. Advanced booking is recommended.

However, there is an optional extension to Cabane Bella Tola, a privately owned refuge set on pastureland with even better views than those from Hôtel Weisshorn, which looks out to the west and north across the Rhône valley to the Bernese Alps. With a magical setting and a very fine route to the Meidpass and Gruben next day, this is an option well worth considering.

Follow directions given in Stage 11 (Zinal – Forcletta – Gruben) to **Alpage Nava** (2340m, 2hr 20min). Ignore the

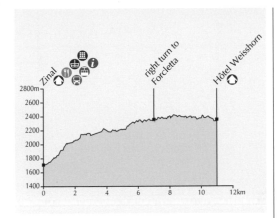

The southern panorama grows even more impressive and includes the Zinalrothorn, the upper chisel-shaped summit of the Matterhorn and Dent Blanche, and it's worth having plenty of halts to enjoy these views.

path breaking off to the right (to the Forcletta) and continue ahead (the sign here gives 1hr to Hôtel Weisshorn), curving round the combe of Montagne de Nava, crossing a few more streams and rising steadily. In early summer the slopes are lavish with alpine flowers. ▶

Autumn colours the hillside on the trail to the Barneuza alpage

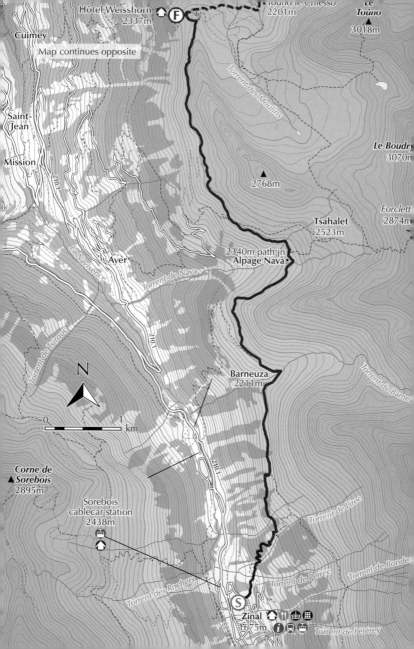

Cuimey

Hôtel Weisshorn ⌂Ⓕ
2337m

Tuûno le Chiesso
2201m

Le Toûno ▲
3018m

Map continues opposite

Saint-
Jean

Mission

2101

Le Boudry
3070m

Torrent des Moulins

2768m ▲

Tsahalet
2523m

Forclett
2874m

2340m path jn
Alpage Nava

Ayer

Torrent de Nava

2101

N

0   1
km

Barneuza
2211m

Torrent de Barne

Corne de
▲ Sorebois
2895m

Torrent de Tsirouc

2101

Torrent de Lirec

Sorebois
cablecar station
2438m

Torrent de Perrese

Torrent de Bonde

Torrent des Rochers

Ⓢ
Zinal ⌂
1675m

Torrent de Pétérey

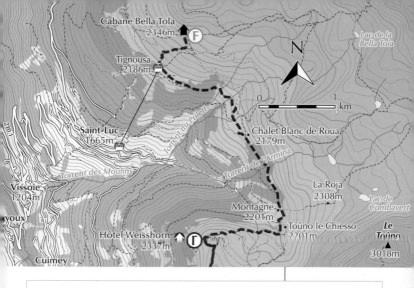

We were on course for setting a record for the slowest-ever walk from Zinal to Hôtel Weisshorn. Our day had become like Morse code, a succession of dots and dashes as we stumbled along the path among autumn-tinged bilberry leaves now blazing scarlet. Progress was painfully slow, for we had to keep turning to where the southern horizon was an upthrust of spires and domes, a patchwork of grey rock and unmarked snow, of gleaming ice and deep blue shadow. Down below the valley had been brushed with early frost that sparkled as it turned to moisture. Now vegetation had dried in the sunlight, and dark swathes of forest lapped against the lower hillside. Bare grass textured the upper levels with velvet. Then rock, snow and ice appeared far off. The head of the valley was the birthplace of glaciers, and all down Val d'Anniviers we could see a tribute to their industry. It was all too good to ignore, and there could be no haste to this day.

This route between Zinal and Hôtel Weisshorn is used in a **mountain marathon** that takes place each summer between Sierre in the Rhône valley and Zinal. The yellow-painted letter Z, which appears at many junctions, is a route guide for this race. Not only is it the full marathon distance of over 26 miles (42km), but the amount of height gain is impressive too. Sierre lies at around 550m above sea level, while sections of the path between Hôtel Weisshorn and Zinal are at more than 2400m.

About 10min from Alpage Nava, at the Bella Lé junction another path cuts to the right to the Forcletta; another descends to Ayer, but we continue straight ahead. Rising still, you come onto a gravel track, but leave it a few paces later for a footpath running parallel with it, but at a higher level. On coming to a second track walk along it for about 200 metres, during which it becomes obvious that this forms part of an avalanche defence system. After a further 200 metres leave the track for a footpath rising above it.

The trail rises and falls across an undulating hillside and soon brings you in sight of the hotel, while an interesting mountain basin is seen off to the right. Shortly after this the path is safeguarded with a fixed chain handrail. You then dip into and through rocky grooves and gullies, then up a rib flanked by bilberries and onto a broad track, where you bear left to reach **Hôtel Weisshorn** (3hr 30min).

HÔTEL WEISSHORN (2337m) 37 beds (half-board only), restaurant service, open June to mid-October. Contact: Hôtel Weisshorn, 3961 St Luc (tel 027 475 11 06, www.weisshorn.ch) – reservation recommended, particularly over weekends when you should book well ahead.

The large, imposing building of the **Hôtel Weisshorn** dates from 1882, and has become something of an institution. Set in a magnificent position more than 1000m above the valley bed, it has the Rhône valley to the north, with the chain of the Bernese Alps rising above that. Sunset views are especially fine. The hotel is popular for wedding parties and other celebrations. The surrounding area is populated with sculptures on an astromonical theme.

Hôtel Weisshorn to Cabane Bella Tola

Walk past Hôtel Weisshorn and take a red–white way-marked path ahead, from which you look down onto St-Luc. When the path forks 2min later take the lower option, shortly after which you curve round the edge of a rocky bluff and continue across bilberry and juniper slopes with a view through the combe of Montagne du Roua, at the head of which lies the Meidpass.

Hôtel Weisshorn is a famous mountain inn, with views across the Rhône valley to the Bernese Alps

The way angles down to a grass basin, where you keep ahead at two junctions then go up a slope and onto a track to the farm of **Toûno le Chiesso** (2201m). Turn left along the track/farm road, and when it forks (25min from Hôtel Weisshorn) keep ahead on the upper branch. About 10min later a sign for Cabane Bella Tola directs you up a path on the right. This contours just above the track, then forks. Take the upper path, which brings you above the farm of **Chalet Blanc de Roua** (2179m).

Ignore the sign to Bella Tola, which refers to the peak and not the cabane, and go ahead on a narrow path that brings you onto a grass track with occasional waymarks. Rising gently, this curves round the hillside, and 1hr 15min from Hôtel Weisshorn a waymark on the left sends

Cabane Bella Tola, a cosy hut in a pastureland setting with amazing views

you up the slope on a path which brings you directly to **Cabane Bella Tola** (5hr).

CABANE BELLA TOLA (2346m) 92 dortoir places, full meals service, open end of June to mid-September (tel 027 476 15 67, http://cabanebellatola.ch).

Owned by the St-Luc/Tignousa funicular company, the **Cabane Bella Tola** is a comfortable refuge with magnificent views. From its pastureland setting it looks south towards the head of Val de Zinal. Hôtel Weisshorn can be seen in the middle distance, but beyond that Weisshorn, Zinalrothorn, Matterhorn and Dent Blanche rim the horizon. Behind the refuge rises the 3025m Bella Tola, claimed by some to be the best viewpoint in the Alps, which is reached from the hut by an easy path in a little under 2hr 30min. The route to the Meidpass on Stage 11B passes directly beneath the Bella Tola peak.

STAGE 11B

*Hôtel Weisshorn/Cabane Bella Tola –
Meidpass – Gruben*

Start	Hôtel Weisshorn/Cabane Bella Tola (2337m/2346m)
Distance	11km (12km from Cab. Bella Tola)
Total ascent	600m (700m)
Total descent	1120m (1220m)
Time	4hr (or 4hr 15min)
High point	Meidpass (2790m)
Accommodation	Gruben: hotel (beds and matratzenlager/dortoir)
Transport options	None

This undemanding day's walk leads out of French-speaking Valais and into German-speaking Wallis – the same canton but linguistically a world apart from that you've been walking through since crossing the Col de Balme.

And it's not just the language that changes either, for a different set of landscapes are in view. On leaving Hôtel Weisshorn the way leads through a curiously contorted country en route to the Meidpass (or Meiden Pass as it is also known), while the way down to the Turtmanntal is a descent into the past. The Turtmanntal seems not to belong to the present century – there is a motor road, it is true, and the Hotel Schwarzhorn has all modern amenities, yet a profound sense of peace prevails, and the valley appears to remain untouched by pressures from the 'outside world'. It is only occupied for part of the year.

The Meidpass route is both direct and interesting, with wonderful views from the actual pass. Whether you begin at Hôtel Weisshorn or Cabane Bella Tola, the approach to the pass (the two routes combine 30min below it) will be inspiring, yet both could challenge your route-finding skills in misty conditions, as there are sections without a visible path. Waymarks or cairns will be your guide.

Out of the hotel turn left where a sign gives 2hr to the Meidpass. Cross a broad track onto a path (waymarked red–white) from which you look onto St-Luc. When the

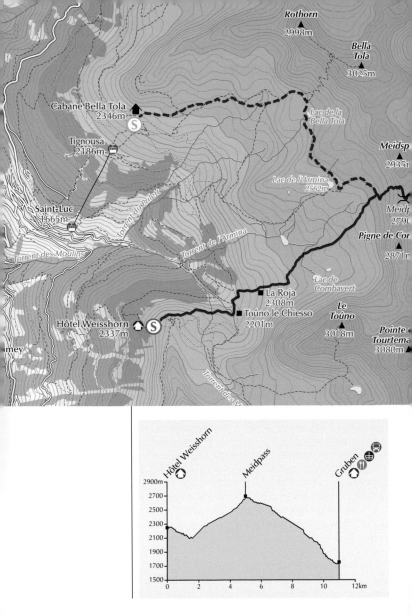

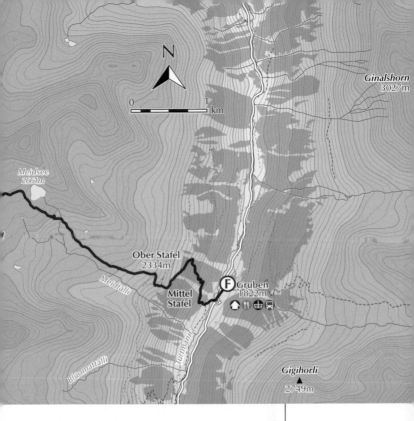

path forks in 2min take the lower option, then curve round the edge of a rocky bluff to gain a view ahead through the combe of Montagne de Roua to the Meidpass. The path angles downhill into a grass basin where you go ahead at two junctions, walk up a slope and continue on a track to the farm of **Toûno le Chiesso** (2201m, 25min).

Take the minor track that goes up the right-hand side of the farm, takes you between buildings then curves right to climb the steep slope above the farm, with craggy shapes appearing in the skyline ahead. The track forks 12min above the farm, where you veer right to approach the solitary building of **La Roja** (2308m), which stands within a walled enclosure. A path skirts this and brings you to a signpost. Bear left and wind up the slope through rough pastures mattressed with juniper, alpenrose and bilberry.

Crossing and recrossing streams, pass a tiny pool, from where spiky fingers of rock are seen on the ridge above, and there are distant views of the Bernese Alps to the north. In 1hr there's a signed junction where the right-hand path offers a 5min diversion (plus 5min back) along a contouring path to visit **Lac de Combavert**, lying at the foot of a great scree chute spilling from Le Toûno.

Continue up the slope to enter a broader pasture-land. As you progress, the path veers a little to the left (north-eastwards) and rises more steeply to meet a stream where it tumbles from an upper basin, which you reach in 1hr 15min. Where you cross the stream a blue painted sign on a rock directs a route left to 'Lac' – this goes to Lac de l'Armina. Ignore this and head north-east towards the peak of Corne du Boeuf (Meidspitz), below which

The mountain and moorland landscape below the Meidpass

you should be able to see a path zig-zagging to the saddle of the Meidpass.

The landscape becomes more rocky now, but the path is well defined. A few minutes later it crosses another little stream, keeps company with it, then recrosses to its right-hand side by another junction (1hr 30min). The left-hand path is the route joining from Cabane Bella Tola; you turn right for the Meidpass.

Cabane Bella Tola to the Meidpass
Immediately behind the refuge a sign indicates the route to Lac de la Bella Tola. Walk along this path, which rises easily over pastures, goes beneath a ski lift and in 10min brings you onto a sort of plateau with a farm track scouring through it. Remain on the path for now, but when you come onto the track near another ski tow, walk along it for about 150 metres until a waymark sends you ahead along the continuing path.

Rising above the track, turn a rocky corner and enter a lovely basin of pasture with a small reedy tarn in it. Keeping left of the tarn, cross a couple of streams feeding into it, then go over more pastures to regain the track. Turn left, and 10min later bear right while the path to climb Bella Tola goes straight ahead. In another 2min the track forks; take the right branch and come to the little **Lac de la Bella Tola** (50min).

Immediately after crossing the lake's outflow stream the track forks again. Bear right, and very shortly after take a waymarked path on the left to rise over a rocky slope with a few cairns and waymarks to guide you as you cross a spur of rock and grass. After passing beneath another ski tow the path curves left and you gain a first view of the Meidpass; below can be seen **Lac de l'Armina** (2562m).

Descend a little to pass along the north-east side of the lake, and at its far side the path curves left to climb a grass slope, where it is joined by a second path (blue–white waymarks) coming from St-Luc. The route is now waymarked both red–white and blue–white as you climb the slope, and is mostly easy to follow, but in misty conditions concentration will be needed.

Rising eastward make towards the south side of Corne du Boeuf (Meidspitz) before curving to the right when the slope levels out. You then descend a little, cross two brief rock tips and, 15min from Lac de l'Armina, come to a signed junction below the Meidpass, where you join the path from Hôtel Weisshorn (1hr 45min).

With a few twists the path takes you up into a very stony hollow, goes up its left-hand side, negotiates a scree and rock slope above it, then takes long and gently angled zig-zags across the final approach to the **Meidpass** (2790m, 2hr) – a narrow stony saddle slung between Corne du Boeuf (Meidspitz) to the north and the tower of Pigne de Combavert to the south.

Just before reaching the pass you gaze back to the distant Mont Blanc de Cheilon, Grand Combin and even Mont Blanc itself. But to the south-east a stony waste-land is buttressed by the lumpy Meidhorn, like the turret of some medieval castle, beyond which gleams the

The Meidpass

Weisshorn. Once again this great mountain looks magnificent, the dominant feature in a wild scene of snow-peaks, glaciers and rock.

The path descends easily, albeit a little steeply at first, winding down into the stony basin and keeping to its left-hand side; the basin itself is rimmed with gesticulating fingers of rock with screes spilling below them. Pass to the right of the **Meidsee** (2661m), after which the path descends to pastureland with a couple of small tarns in it.

Looking ahead at the Meidpass, the Weisshorn rises high above the Turtmann and Mattertal valleys

There was no wind, no breeze, no sound of streams or falling stones, nor of marmot, sheep or cowbell. We were both so struck by the overpowering sense of peace and stillness that we stopped for a minute and listened. And it was true. It was as though even the Earth itself had ceased to spin; as though all and everything had momentarily been frozen in time. There were no sounds. Before I had always believed that so long as there was life there could be no such thing as silence – there would be some semblance of sound, if only the hum of distance. But this was the nearest I had ever come to total soundlessness. We'd entered a zone of silence.

The path leads to the alp hamlet of **Ober Stafel** – the 'upper alp' at 2334m where you come onto a track. A few paces along this leave it for a continuing path which descends steeply to the lower alp (**Mittel Stafel**), with its view upvalley to the Turtmann glacier, off to the left to the glaciers of Wildstrubel and Balmhorn in the Bernese Alps, and to the cone of the lovely Bietschhorn which rises above the Lötschental on the far side of the unseen Rhône valley.

The impressive and very difficult **Bietschhorn** ('whose attractions are so overwhelming that it cannot escape perpetual attraction' – according to RLG Irving) is seen to the north in the line of the Bernese Alps. An isolated mountain of 3934m, it stands high above the tranquil Lötschental, which it dominates by its powerful presence. It was first climbed by Leslie Stephen and his guides on 13 August 1859.

A narrow path takes you through the hamlet of chalets and barns (water supply), then descends another steep grass slope before angling gently to the left to enter a forest of stone pine and larch. This brings you down to the valley floor. Cross the **Turtmänna** stream by a bridge and walk up the opposite slope to reach the small village of **Gruben** (1822m, 4hr). For details see notes at the end of Stage 11.

STAGE 12
Gruben – Augstbordpass – St Niklaus

Start	Gruben (1822m)
Distance	18km
Total ascent	1150m
Total descent	1850m
Time	7hr
High point	Augstbordpass (2894m)
Accommodation	St Niklaus: hotels, pensions
Transport options	cablecar (Jungen–St Niklaus)

This stage is one of the finest of them all, and a walk to stand comparison with almost any other day's outing in the Pennine Alps. It has so many contrasts, so many features that capture one's attention. It has history too, for the Augstbordpass which links the Turtmanntal with the Mattertal was used from the Middle Ages onward as an important trading route between the Rhône valley and Italy – a route that originally continued from St Niklaus to Zermatt and over the glacial Theodule Pass beside the Matterhorn.

Crossing the final pass on the Chamonix to Zermatt route is a highlight in every sense of the word. Never as demanding as the total height gain and loss might suggest, it leads through spacious woodland, over high pastures and into a stony wilderness, but then opens to some of the loveliest views in all Switzerland. The Matterhorn does not feature in these views, however, but remains hidden until you are committed to the Europaweg on the far side of the Mattertal. But other high peaks – most notably the Dom (the highest peak entirely within Swiss territory) – add much to the scene, while the Mattertal itself appears as an incredibly deep trench of greenery walled by grey rock and forest another world away.

Then comes the descent into that world, and this too is full of pleasures and the odd surprise – none greater or more beautiful than the discovery of the little hamlet of Jungen clinging to the desperately steep mountain slopes high above St Niklaus. Not an unreal tourist haunt, this is a living, working, daily active alp hamlet, and one of the last such remote farming communities to be met on the Walker's Haute Route, although in recent years even Jungen seems to have undergone a level of 'gentrification'.

From Jungen the path plunges once again into forest, dropping into the shadowed depths of the Mattertal past a series of tiny white shrines as views of the valley are rearranged with almost every step.

The way to the Augstbordpass begins on the south side of Hotel Schwarzhorn, where a grassy trail heads straight up the slope towards sparse woods of larch and pine. This soon becomes a generous path with long weaving zig-zags on which you gain height without too much effort.

In a little under an hour you will arrive at the four-way path junction of **Grüobualp** (2151m). Ignore alternatives and continue uphill (the right-hand option goes to the Turtmann Hut). Emerging from the woods, about 15min from the Grüobualp junction, come onto the remains of a dirt road created to service the construction of an avalanche defence system. The hillside has been mostly reinstated now, and you bear right along what appears to

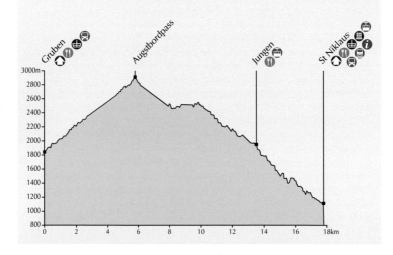

be a slightly broader path which soon cuts up to the left and offers a view of the avalanche defences. The continuing climb winds up to an open shelf occupied by the two alp buildings of **Ober Grüobu Stafel** (2369m, 1hr 20min) with wide views across the valley to the Meidpass.

Passing to the right of the huts the path continues uphill to the left of a stream in the hanging valley of Grüobtälli. The path later crosses and recrosses this stream, and there are no unduly steep sections as you rise to a lumpy inner region with screes lining the southern wall of peaks, and grassy hummocks elsewhere littered with grey-green lichened rocks. As with the basin below the Meidpass, this area too is a place where few sounds intrude on a windless day.

After about 2hr 30min the trail steepens as you rise over a rocky step, then descend slightly to skirt a small pond before curving left and rising again, this time at a steady incline across boulders on the final stretch to the **Augstbordpass** (2894m, 3hr).

The pass overlooks a wild and rock-strewn wilderness, a landscape of austere beauty. Ahead in the distance rises the pointed, glacier-draped Fletschhorn

Rockbound pool below the Augstbordpass

191

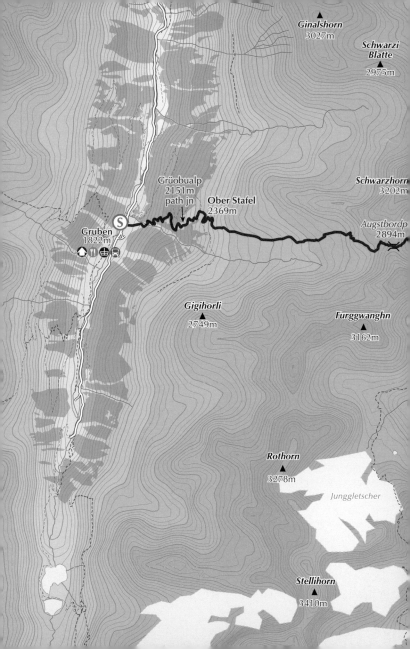

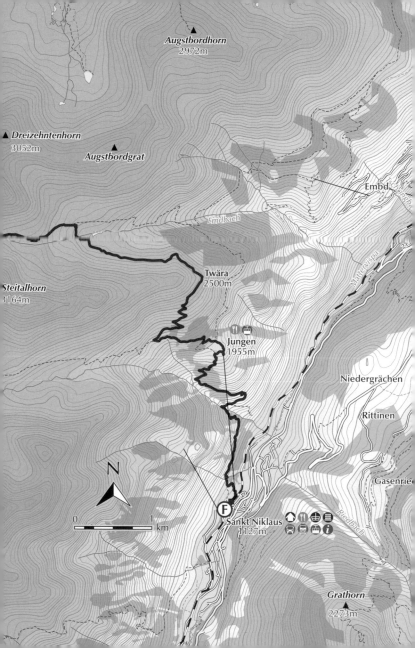

(3985m) above the vague hint of the Saastal, while in the middle distance northern outliers of the great Mischabel wall, with Balfrin and Ulrichshorn above the Ried glacier, spread in a lavish show of grandeur.

FLETSCHHORN

Rising high above the village of Saas Balen in the Saastal, the Fletschhorn (3985m) is a mountain of some complexity and one which, though little known outside climbing circles, commands a certain respect. Its twisted ridges ensure that every view of it is different. Glaciers sweep down on each side between extended rocky spurs. Immediately to the south is the Lagginhorn, with the Boshorn to the north. The Fletschhorn received its first ascent in 1854.

Given sufficient time, energy and inclination, the **Schwarzhorn** (3201m) to the north of the pass would be worth a visit (1hr from the pass by path most of the way). The summit has the reputation of being one of the great viewpoints of the Alps. The panorama is 'one of surpassing magnificence': to the north is a memorable spread of the Bernese Alps, including Finsteraarhorn and Doldenhorn; to the south the view takes in Monte Rosa, Liskamm, Weisshorn and Dent Blanche; and to the east the Ticino Alps blaze a blue horizon, while nearer

MISCHABEL

Mischabel is the name given to that huge wall of peaks that forms the western section of Saas Fee's noted amphitheatre and makes an effective divide between the Saastal and the Mattertal. The Mischabel wall consists of Täschhorn, Dom and Lenzspitze, with a spur going north-west to include the Nadelhorn. It's a consistently high wall whose crest nowhere falls below 4000m. A bivouac hut stands on the Mischabeljoch at the southern end, while the Mischabel huts (there are two) are perched on a rib of rock between the Hohbalm and smaller Fall glaciers. The western flanks are served by the Täsch, Kin, Dom and Bordier huts. Only the northern outliers of the Mischabel group are seen at first from the Augstbordpass.

to hand rise the Mischabel chain, Weissmies, Fletschhorn and Monte Leone.

From the Augstbordpass a clear path drops in zig-zags to a stony bowl on the eastern side – the cirque that cups the Inners Tälli. Progressing steeply at first, the way eases lower down, and 25min from the pass emerges onto scant grass littered with rocks. About 10min later you come to a junction of paths, taking the right-hand option (signed to Jungen and St Niklaus) that slopes down and then veers over to the right-hand side of the valley after crossing the **Emdbach** stream.

The route now embarks on a gently rising traverse of the southern flank of the valley, heading east across a slope of boulders and rocks. But it's a well-made path in the circumstances which brings you to a shoulder at

Mattertal and the Ried glacier from the Twära viewpoint

2488m, where you gain a first sighting of the deep cut of the Mattertal. Off to the left can be seen the Grosser Aletschgletscher.

THE MATTERTAL AND THE GROSSER ALETSCHGLETSCHER

The Vispertal strikes south from the Rhône valley for 7km to Stalden, where it forks. To the south-east lies the Saastal, cut by the Saaservispa river, while south-westward runs the Mattertal, the valley of the Mattervispa river. At its head lies Zermatt, with the Matterhorn towering over it. The **Mattertal** is a narrow, deeply cut valley flanked by the highest peaks in Switzerland. The eastern wall is that of the Mischabelhörner (see above); the western wall contains such magnificent peaks as Zinalrothorn, Schalihorn, Weisshorn, Bishorn and Brunegghorn; while the valley is blocked in the south by the glacier-hung mountains that run westward from Monte Rosa – Liskamm, Castor, Pollux, Breithorn and Matterhorn.

Seen to the north as a great ice river on the far side of the Rhône valley, the **Grosser Aletschgletscher** is the longest glacier in the Alps. It flows for some 23km, draining such Oberland peaks as Mittaghorn, Gletscherhorn, Jungfrau, Mönch and Fiescherhorn. Some very fine walks, accessible from Riederalp, Bettmeralp or Kühboden, may be had on footpaths that run alongside the lower reaches of this glacier. (See *Walking in the Valais* by Kev Reynolds, a walking guide also published by Cicerone Press.)

Continuing round the mountainside the path narrows and is exposed in places (**care required**). It climbs one or two rock steps then turns a spur (**Twära** 2500m, 45min), and there before you is one of those rare sights that is so overwhelmingly powerful that all else is forgotten. Across the gulf of the Mattertal soar Nadelhorn, Lenzspitze and Dom, with the Ried glacier pouring into the shoehorn trough it has carved above Grächen's green terrace. It is a stunning vision, full of drama and grace of form, a perfect symbol of mountain architecture. Then, right at the head of the Mattertal, are Liskamm, Castor and Pollux and the long white block of the Breithorn, with the smaller pyramid of the Klein Matterhorn next to it. (The Matterhorn itself remains shyly hidden behind the black outline of the Mettelhorn.)

THE DOM

At 4545m the Dom is the highest individual mountain in Switzerland, since the Dufourspitze on Monte Rosa (4634m) is shared with Italy. The summit tops the Mischabel wall. From it the Festi glacier flows steeply westward, while the Hohberggletscher falls to the north-west and is fed by the neighbouring Lenzspitze and Nadelhorn. The normal ascent route from the Dom Hut follows the right bank of the Festigletscher, crosses the Festijoch and then makes a broad sweep up the head of the Hohberggletscher towards the summit. The Dom was first climbed in 1858, and received an early ski ascent (by Arnold Lunn and Joseph Knubel) in 1917.

A few more paces and, most stunning of all, the Weisshorn yet again announces its domineering presence above and behind the Brunegghorn that rises in one immense shaft nearly 2500m out of the valley. ▶

Beyond the viewpoint the route follows a paved mule-path for a short distance on huge flat slabs, before you descend steeply on a footpath with a view into the Jungtal hanging valley. With numerous twists the path leads down the very steep grass hillside to another junction. Continue ahead towards the first larch trees; 3min later come to the Unterer Läger junction at 2255m and turn right. At yet another junction by a drystone wall you catch sight of Jungen and follow the trail towards it.

This spur of mountainside is surely the crowning glory of the Walker's Haute Route, a route that presents one visual gem after another from start to finish.

Jungen hangs on a small pasture above the Mattertal

Through larchwoods the path splits into several braidings, but these reunite just before you enter the hamlet of

JUNGEN (1955M, 5HR 30MIN)

Perched on a steep slope of mountainside 900m above the Mattertal, with which it is linked by cableway, Jungen is a delightful collection of old timber chalets and haybarns, with a white-painted chapel and two restaurants, the Junger-Stübli and the Bergrestaurant Jungeralp near the cablecar station. In the early summer cheese is made in a building at the western entrance to the hamlet, but when the cattle are moved up into the Jungtal the cheesemaker goes with them. A very fine high route, the Moosalp–Jungen Höhenweg, roughly follows the 2000m contour north-east for about 9km. (**Note** The LS map and some others name this hamlet Jungu.)

As soon as we saw the hamlet from the path way above it, we knew instinctively that it would offer something special, and it did. Coming down to Jungen reinforced that initial instinct. First there was the visual dimension – a quintessential alp hamlet of almost black timbers with a long, dramatic view to the head of the valley. The valley lay 900m below; the Dom (4545m) soared up to full height opposite, a white crust above the rocky Grubenhorn, with the Ried glacier peeling through its funnel; Brunegghorn and Weisshorn above to the right dazzled in the afternoon sunlight. We wandered between the buildings and, just below the chapel, saw a restaurant, the Junger-Stübli, and couldn't resist stopping there for a drink with that view before us. Our original plan had been to continue down to St Niklaus, but when we realised there was a bed to be had here, our plan changed instantly. St Niklaus could wait until tomorrow. That evening we studied the mountains through binoculars, noting the light of the Bordier Hut opposite below the Balfrin, and another at the head of the valley where a glow-worm sized train moved slowly against the black mountain shapes towards the Gornergrat – a world remote from ours. Jungen was full of magic and we spent a memorable night there, enjoying first-class hospitality (that has been repeated on every return since) in a setting that is nothing short of pure enchantment. Sadly, accommodation is no longer available in Jungen, but several options exist in St Niklaus.

The path through Jungen leads to the chapel (if you prefer to descend by cablecar turn left at the junction in the middle of the hamlet on a path that goes directly to the cableway station). From the chapel descend steeply and wind in zig-zags into forest. Beside the forest path you will pass a whole series of small white shrines, most of which have been dedicated by Mattertal families.

The steep path between Jungen and St Niklaus is punctuated with small chapels (photo: Madeline Williams)

About 35min below Jungen there's a footpath junction where you continue straight ahead – the alternative trail cuts sharply back to the left. Cross a rocky cleft on a footbridge over the Jungbach stream, beyond which the gradient is less severe. The way winds on, still through forest as it works round the lower hillside, then between small parcels of meadowland to reach the railway station at **St Niklaus** (7hr).

Before deciding on overnight accommodation in St Niklaus consider your onward plan. Should you decide to opt for the high route to Zermatt via the Europaweg

ST NIKLAUS (1127M)

This is the main village of the valley, formerly known as Gassen. St Niklaus has a 17th-century church with an onion-domed spire similar to many seen in the Tyrol. Home to a number of well-known guiding families of the Golden Age and post-Golden Age of Mountaineering, including the Knubels and Pollingers, the village has a mountain guides museum, the Bergführer, Heimat- und Mineralienmuseum (open Tues and Fri, 4–6pm, from mid-July to end of September).

Accommodation, refreshments, shops, banks, PTT, railway (to Zermatt and Visp), cablecar to Jungen, bus to Grächen and Gasenried. Tourist information: Tourismusbüro, 3924 St Niklaus (tel 027 955 60 60, **www.st-niklaus.ch**). Lower-priced accommodation: Hotel La Réserve (tel 027 955 22 55, **www.la-reserve.ch**).

(Stages 13 and 14) you may choose to take the bus to Gasenried (saving an uphill walk of 2hr) in order to tackle the first stage of the Europaweg tomorrow. In this case the bus leaves from just outside St Niklaus railway station. (For accommodation in Gasenried refer to Stage 12A.) However, if you plan to walk the valley route to Zermatt (Stages 13A/14A), your best bet is to overnight in St Niklaus. Before committing yourself to the Europaweg, you are strongly advised to read the notes in the introduction to Stage 13 and check conditions locally, as the route may be closed by stonefall.

OPTIONS BETWEEN ST NIKLAUS AND ZERMATT

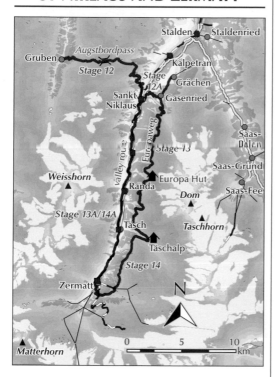

Some time-constrained parties will stop at St Niklaus and take the train to Zermatt, but for the through-trekker the choice is between the two-day **Europaweg** trail and a straightforward **valley walk to Zermatt** in one day. The Europaweg stages are high, stony and have protected sections – full details are given in the information for Stage 13. It includes the crossing of the Charles Kuonen Hängebrücke, a 500-metre suspension bridge built in 2017, reputedly the world's longest of its type. The valley route is full of interest, but cannot compare with the higher route.

A further option, which could also be used if the Stage 13 route is closed, as sometimes happens, would be to take the valley route as far as **Randa** (3hr 45min walking time, 340m ascent) and then climb directly to the Europa Hut (2hr from Randa, 850m ascent). There are waymarked paths either side of the Dorfbachli torrent. The southerly routing comes out to the south of the bridge, which would need to be crossed to reach the hut, while the northerly path does not.

The bridge itself is a wonderfully solid structure and should present few or no objective issues for the trekker, although it will certainly test the resilience to exposure of some as it hangs 80m above the gorge. It's probably best to avoid it in thundery or very windy conditions, but the alternative is to drop nearly to Randa and re-climb the other side.

A final compromise option would be to take the valley route to **Täsch**, then the minibus to Täschalp, either late afternoon or first thing in the morning, to enjoy the higher-level path to Zermatt with constant views of the Matterhorn.

Our recommendation would be to do the Europaweg unless there are reasons otherwise.

STAGE 12A
St Niklaus – Gasenried

Start	St Niklaus (1127m)
Distance	4km
Total ascent	600m
Total descent	70m
Time	2hr
High point	Gasenried (1659m)
Accommodation	Gasenried: hotel with matratzenlager
Transport options	Bus (St Niklaus–Gasenried)
Alternative route	St Niklaus to Grächen

This very short walk is an important linking stage which brings the Haute Route trekker to the start of the two-day Europaweg leading to Zermatt. As mentioned at the end of the previous stage, an alternative option would be to take the bus from St Niklaus to Gasenried – either on arrival at St Niklaus or early next morning – to enable you to set off fresh for the Europa Hut. Since the first stage of the Europaweg leading to the Europa Hut is quite demanding, it would not be advisable to add this (admittedly short) walk to the beginning. Better to have a comfortable night in Gasenried before setting out. There are some pleasant, scenic local walks above the village to help fill the day.

Since there's only one hotel in Gasenried (modestly priced and with matratzenlager) it is advisable to telephone ahead to ensure there are beds available. Should the hotel be fully booked an alternative suggestion is to walk (or take the bus) to Grächen, 30min walk from Gasenried, where there's plenty of accommodation. Walk back to Gasenried for the continuing Europaweg.

From the village square below St Niklaus railway station walk right on Dorfstrasse and then turn left down an alley onto Talstrasse, before crossing over onto the road Eyeweg. This leads to a bridge over both the main valley road and the **Mattervispa river**, which you cross and

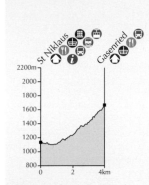

turn left, ignoring the Rundsweg signed right. After passing a number of houses come to the Grächen road about 10min from the start. Cross this and walk up a minor road rising among more houses. It curves to the right and reaches a staggered crossroads. Once again cross over and continue ahead. When the road ends on the edge of woodland a footpath takes the onward route over a stream, then climbs among trees. On emerging from the woods this path makes a rising traverse of the steeply sloping hillside overlooking the northern outskirts of St Niklaus.

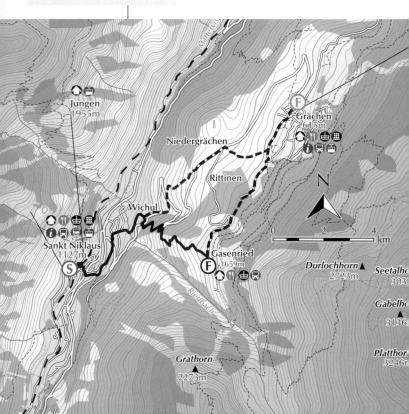

About 25min above St Niklaus you come to the collection of old timber chalets of **Wichul** (1195m) where you bear right onto a narrow road. This curves sharply to the right about 50 metres later.

Detour to Grächen

The route to Grächen slants left, signed 1hr 25min, rising among pinewoods, crosses and recrosses the road on the way to **Rittinen** (1455m, 1hr 15min), then continues via **Niedergrächen** 15min later, where a footpath climbs among chalets and haybarns to reach the attractive resort of **Grächen** (2hr). ▸

From Grächen the onward route to Gasenried begins by the parish church on Dorfplatz and is well signed. It is part of the Europaweg and takes an easy 30min to join Stage 13.

GRÄCHEN (1615M)

Sprawling along a sun-trap of a terrace on the east side of the Mattertal, about 500m above St Niklaus, this very pleasant resort attracts visitors in winter and summer. By judicious use of the Seetalhorn and Hannigalp cableways some tremendous viewpoints are easily accessible, but even without this mechanical aid, numerous footpaths give scenically rewarding walks. There are two classic long walks from here. The first is the **Balfrin Höhenweg** (or Höhenweg Saas Fee as it's also known), which makes a challenging high-level route to Saas Fee by a series of former shepherds' paths, and was opened in 1954. This takes 7–7hr 30min to complete. The other long route is the 31km **Europaweg** (opened July 1997) between Grächen and Zermatt, which now forms the last two stages of the Chamonix to Zermatt Walker's Haute Route. With plenty of accommodation choices, Grächen makes a good base for a walking holiday.

Accommodation, restaurants, shops, banks, PTT, bus (St Niklaus–Grächen). Tourist information: Tourismusbüro, 3925 Grächen (tel 027 955 60 60, **www. graechen.ch**). Lower-priced accommodation: Hotel Alpha (B&B rates plus self-catering facilities (tel 027 956 13 01, **www.alpha-graechen.ch**); Hotel Alpina, 10% discount for Europaweg walkers – password: 'Europaweg-Wanderer Tour Monte-Rosa' (tel 027 955 26 00, **www.hotelalpinagraechen.ch**); Hotel Garni Abendruh (tel 027 956 11 16); Hotel Sonne (tel 027 956 11 07); Hotel Pension Bellevue (tel 027 956 33 30).

Keep to the road until it meets the main Grächen road. Cross over, and 30 metres up the hill the path resumes the climb among woods of larch and pine.

The Ried glacier drains into a valley behind Gasenried

Climbing in fairly steep zig-zags through forest, the way emerges onto the road again. Bear right and turn the hairpin bend, from which you gain a tremendous view upvalley. About 70 metres after the hairpin cut back to the right on a track rising among trees. When it forks soon after by a timber building take the upper route. This winds uphill, and on reaching a four-way path junction with two signs to Gasenried (1hr from St Niklaus) you continue ahead. The next junction is met by a shrine and a crucifix, where you bear right to make a final climb to Gasenried, soon passing between vegetable plots with the village seen above.

The lower part of the village is reached in about 1hr 20min, and from here you gain views north to the Bernese Alps, with the pointed Bietschhorn prominent in that view. Follow a narrow road which rises steeply to the main part of **Gasenried** (2hr) where the Ried glacier is seen at the head of a hanging valley behind the village. The only hotel, the Alpenrösli, is situated in the square near the church. ▶

Grächen is a 30min walk along a clearly marked level track.

GASENRIED (1659M)

This low-key neighbour of Grächen is dug into the steep hillside a little further south. The village stands on two levels and consists of a number of typical Valaisian chalets and granaries, while just above it footpaths cut through steep pastures and forests to extend the views. The valley of the Riedbach torrent lies behind Gasenried, with the Ried glacier hanging in its upper reaches. As a holiday base, Gasenried would suit any walkers not interested in 'night life'. It's a quiet place with lots of opportunities for walkers.

Accommodation, restaurant, shop, PTT, bus (St Niklaus–Gasenried). Tourist information: Tourismusbüro, 3924 St Niklaus (tel 027 956 36 63). Hotel Alpenrösli, 28 beds, 10 matratzenlager places; open June–October (tel 027 956 17 81).

Gasenried at the start of the Europaweg

STAGE 13
Gasenried – Europa Hut

Start	Gasenried (1659m)
Distance	15km
Total ascent	1180m
Total descent	570m
Time	6hr 30min
High point	North of Galenberg (2690m)
Accommodation	Europa Hut: mountain refuge
Transport options	None
Note	The nature of this stage makes timing really quite variable. Strong parties will find these times generous, while less-strong parties may need considerable extra time.
Alternative route	St Niklaus to Zermatt via the Mattertal: see Stage 13A/14A

Created in 1997, the Europaweg is a challenging route stretching well over 30km between Grächen and Zermatt. It climbs high above the Mattertal – as much as 1400m above the valley in some places – with one tremendous viewpoint after another to make it a visual extravaganza virtually from start to finish. One of the best panoramas is enjoyed about two hours after setting out, when the Matterhorn at last reveals itself at the head of the valley. The Bietschhorn is seen in the other direction, Dom and Ried glacier to the south-east, and Weisshorn to the south-west, plus numerous other peaks, each of which would be a major attraction in any other range.

The Europaweg is a tough, challenging but rewarding finale to the Walker's Haute Route, but all who tackle it should only do so after careful consideration of the risks involved. Before setting out, you are strongly advised to telephone ahead to the Europa Hut to book bedspace for the night. In the high season it is likely to be very busy. The website www.europaweg.ch gives frequent updates as to the state of the route and any major diversions in place, and the warden at the Europa Hut is well placed to advise on day-by-day conditions. Read the warning notes before deciding whether this route is for you, or whether to take one of the alternative options described.

IMPORTANT WARNING

It will take a total of 12–14hr to walk these two stages from Gasenried to Zermatt. By far the majority of the Europaweg is as safe as can be expected, but this is a high mountain path, different in character from much of the Walker's Haute Route. The walker is subjected to almost constant exposure and if you don't deal with this well or are less than totally surefooted, you are advised not to attempt the route. There are several places (the first about 2hr 30min from Gasenried) that are potentially dangerous from stonefall or other objective hazards where walkers are urged to be extra vigilant and to move quickly over the danger areas. There are countless sections safeguarded with lengths of fixed rope, too. The Europaweg, which is publicised as part of the Tour of Monte Rosa and also forms a section of the Tour of the Matterhorn, has become extremely popular, but everyone who tackles it should make his or her own judgement whether the risks outlined here (and marked with warning signs on the trail itself) are worth taking. Should you think not, then either follow the alternative one-day valley route described as Stage 13A/14A to Zermatt, or take a train from St Niklaus to Randa and climb directly to the Europa Hut, so tackling the less rockfall-prone Stage 14 and enjoying the delights of the 500-metre bridge.

The unstable nature of the Europaweg cannot be overstated. Of all stages of the Walker's Haute Route, the route of the Europaweg is particularly vulnerable to change; heavy rains, snowmelt, frost and the general instability of the mountain environment can all have an effect, and it is likely that some sections described here will be different by the time you come to tackle them. Where the path is different from that described, please follow Europaweg signs which should indicate the current route.

Follow the road past the church in Gasenried curving left into the Riedbach valley. On reaching a small chapel the road forks. Take the lower option, which becomes a track leading past a picnic area to a bridge spanning the **Riedbach** torrent. Over the bridge immediately turn left on a path which climbs steeply for a few minutes, then, at a poorly marked junction, contours to the right through woodland. Before long the path climbs again, twisting uphill, steeply most of the time, and with the way clearly signed at all junctions.

Gasenried
1659m

S

Sankt Niklaus
1127m

Durlochhorn
2723m

Riedbach

Gabelhorn
3136m

Platth
324

Grathorn
2273m
Grat
2300m

N

Mittelberg
2718m

Färichhorn
3292m

Grosse Graben

Bigergle
Kle
Biger
318

Breithorn
3178m

Riedgletscher

Gugla
3377m

Herbriggen
1263m

Riedgletsch

Galenberg 2581m path jn

Chli
Dirruhorn
3890m

Gelsstriftbach

Dirrugletscher

Dürrenhorn
4035m

Birchbach

Hobärggletscher

Hohbergho
4219m

Map continues opposite

0   1
km

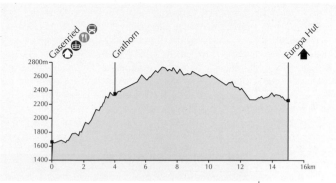

As you gain height occasional views are glimpsed through the trees to the Bietschhorn in the distance and Gasenried below. In 1hr 50min reach a viewpoint (**Grat 2300m**) with a stunning panorama that concentrates on the chain of the Bernese Alps and the gleaming Grosser Aletschgletscher, while through a gap spikey peaks on the west side of the Mattertal will be recognised as being on show on the descent into the Turtmanntal from the Forcletta on Stage 11; the most conspicuous of these is

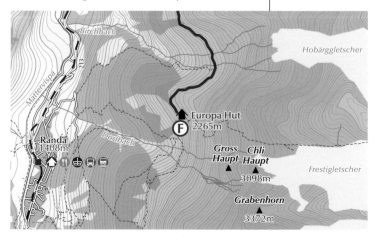

211

the 3411m Gässispitz. Just above the viewpoint a large cross extends the view and makes a very fine belvedere.

The path now curves through the rocky gap to a view of the Barrhorn and Weisshorn, and 5min later you gain another wonderful viewpoint at 2335m, marked by a signpost, from where the unmistakable Matterhorn can be seen upvalley. Bear left and climb higher up the ridge, guided by waymarks and cairns, to emerge onto a broad open shoulder on which there's a statue of St Bernard off to the left (2460m, 2hr 15min). ◀

From this point the Riedgletscher is seen to good effect to the south-east – the Bordier Hut can also be seen from here on the east bank of the glacier.

This statue of St Bernard stands just above the Grat viewpoint

The statue of **St Bernard** on the viewpoint of the Mittelberg ridge commemorates the opening of the Europaweg in 1997. This patron saint of mountain travellers was formerly Archdeacon of Aosta, Bernard of Menthon, who spent many years caring for travellers and pilgrims in trouble after crossing the alpine pass named after him, and who was responsible for the construction of the original hospice there. Bernard died in the 1080s and was beatified shortly after. In 1923 Pope Pius XI confirmed St Bernard as patron saint of the Alps.

The Europaweg continues to rise, crossing a rocky area to another path junction, where you continue straight ahead. Here the trail has been forced across a very rough slope, and about 2hr 30min from Gasenried you reach the first major challenges of boulders, exposed scree and particularly stonefall in the **Grosse Graben** combe. **Much of this combe is in an unstable condition, and signs warn trekkers to cross the danger areas quickly.** A combination of caution and speed is advised.

Stonefall danger area in the Grosse Graben combe

On the south side of the combe beneath the Breithorn there are several fixed rope sections, then on rounding a rocky spur at about 2690m you reach the highest part of the Europaweg and gain yet more stunning views of the Weisshorn. The way then descends a little, before zig-zagging up to pass round another spur and contour to a wooden walkway followed by another fixed rope section (4hr). At this point the greatest difficulties are behind you. Just beyond this another signpost gives 35min to Galenberg and 1hr 50min to the hut (a tough challenge).

Flanking the Ried glacier the **Breithorn** (3178m) forms part of the long north-west arête running down from the Nadelhorn, and is just one of many mountains in the Swiss Alps to bear this name, which means, literally, 'broad mountain'. Perhaps the best known of the Breithorns is that which carries the Swiss/Italian border above Zermatt. Others of note are the Lauterbrunnen Breithorn and Lötschental Breithorn, and there's another above the Simplon Pass not far from Monte Leone.

Views now include the snowy mass of the Zermatt Breithorn at the head of the valley on the border with Italy. There follows another lengthy fixed rope section, and in 4hr 45min you come to the **Galenberg junction** (2581m) where one path descends to Herbriggen, which lies in the valley midway between St Niklaus and Randa (a 2hr descent). At this junction take the upper path ahead, now with a clear view across the valley to the site of a massive rockfall above Randa. The route contours round a huge and steep valley; after rising a little the path loops down to lose about 250m of height and reaches yet another path junction (5hr 30min). The Europa Hut is signed 45min.

In April 1991 a massive **rockfall** reshaped the mountainside north-west of Randa when a vast section of the Langenflueberg collapsed into the valley, demolishing the railway, blocking the river and cutting off the upper Mattertal for several days.

The way curves into a hillside 'bay' overhung by séracs of the Hobärg glacier. There is some minor danger of falling ice, and for a short stretch there are warning signs by the path. Crossing glacial streams, first on a wooden bridge, then a small bridge (that avoids the stream bed under wet conditions), shortly followed by a 30-metre suspension bridge over a deep gully (cross with care), the way contours round the south side of the 'bay' and comes to the Miesboden spur (2280m), another splendid viewpoint. From here the path twists down among a few larches to reach the **Europa Hut** (6hr 30min).

The Europa Hut, overnight halt on the Europaweg

EUROPA HUT (2265m) staffed from mid-June to mid-October, 42 places, full meals service (tel 027 967 82 47, **www.europaweg.ch**). The hut is a fine timber-built refuge, opened in 1999, with views directly across the valley to the Weisshorn and upvalley to the Breithorn, Klein Matterhorn, Mettelhorn and Schalihorn.

STAGE 14
Europa Hut – Täschalp – Zermatt

Start	Europa Hut (2265m)
Distance	23km
Total ascent	850m
Total descent	1510m
Time	7hr
High point	Sunnegga (2288m) and 2350m high point on path 4km before Sunnegga
Accommodation	Täschalp (Ottavan) (3hr 30min): matratzenlager; Zermatt: hotels, pensions, matratzenlager, youth hostel, camping
Transport options	Sunnegga Express funicular (Sunnegga–Zermatt); bus (Winkelmatten–Zermatt)

This is a long final stage, with many fine viewpoints along the route and several kilometres of rope or cable protecting sections that are somewhat exposed, but to a trekker who has followed the whole Chamonix–Zermatt trail these sections should present few challenges. Views and fine walking apart, the highlight is the new Charles Kuonen Hängebrücke, a 500-metre suspension bridge 20min into the stage. This phenomenal engineering achievement replaced the previous 250-metre bridge that was destroyed by rockfall in 2013 shortly after its construction, and saves an 800m descent nearly to Randa and re-ascent. The bridge crosses the Dorfbach chasm, which is overlooked by the west flank glaciers of the Dom, Lenzspitz and Nadelhorn and their rocky remains; this new bridge seems very well-built but if it too is destroyed (hard to imagine) then rerouting would again be necessary. Given the somewhat exposed nature of the first 2hr walking towards Täschalp, other reroutings are possible, although less likely.

It's a long last day, but wonderful, assuming good weather. Early in the day the Weisshorn dominates the view, around Täsch the Zinalrothorn draws eye and attention, but throughout the day the emerging status of the Matterhorn, looming high above Zermatt takes the lead. Refreshment opportunities at Täschalp, Tufteren and Sunnegga allow the trekker to relax and take it all in. The Chamonix–Zermatt route is coming to a spectacular conclusion.

For up-to-date information about the state of the trail to Zermatt, enquire at the Europa Hut.

On leaving the Europa Hut the path slopes downhill and 5min later comes to a junction with the Dom Hut path. Continue to descend, and in another 5min a second junction (Domhüttenweg 2149m) directs the Europaweg straight ahead, while the alternative path descends to Randa.

The way now slants down to the start of the Charles Kuonen bridge at 2065m. The bridge spans about 500 metres, single file. Passing walkers headed in the other direction presents few problems. So substantial are the

500 metres is a long way, but the bridge is very solidly built

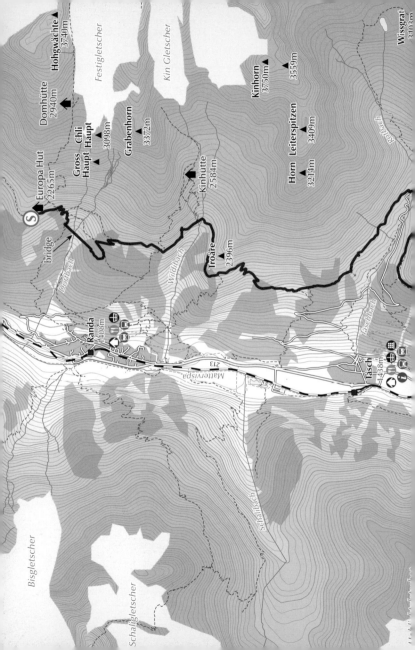

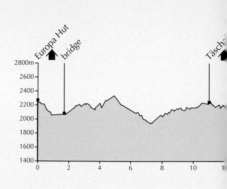

cables and fixings that this bridge seems significantly more solid that many other mountain bridges (and indeed much of the Europaweg) and the trekker should not be deterred by its looming presence, perhaps felt many days before it is reached.

After the bridge (45min), pass through sparse larch-woods and come to yet another path junction with a second descent option to Randa. On emerging from the woods the Matterhorn comes into view ahead.

THE MATTERHORN

Standing on the borders of Switzerland and Italy like some gigantic frontier post, at 4478m the Matterhorn is the most easily recognised of all Alpine peaks, its distinctive pyramid shape having been adopted as the very symbol of Switzerland. Not unnaturally it is the focus of attention of practically every visitor to Zermatt, and there can be few mountain activists who do not, at some time or another, feel a longing to climb it. Edward Whymper's obsession has been shared by many in the 150-odd years that have passed since his first ascent on 14 July 1865 which, with its subsequent tragedy, has passed into history as one of the best known of all mountaineering stories. Zermatt's Alpine Museum is the place to visit if you have an interest in this story.

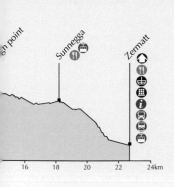

About 40min from the hut a long uphill section of fixed ropes leads to more larchwoods and a sign to the Kinhütte. Our path descends a little and shortly turns a spur to enter the Wildikin combe. It is here that the path has been engineered through a tunnel about 100 metres long (although there are solar-powered lights, a headtorch may be useful). Out of the tunnel a steel footbridge spans the **Wildibach** torrent draining the Kingletscher, then the path curves round the south side of the combe and leaves it by turning a spur, 1hr 30min from the Europa Hut.

Now the Matterhorn, Klein Matterhorn and Breithorn provide a focus at the head of the valley. Ignoring another descent option to Randa, the Europaweg makes a winding descent of the west flank of the Leiterspitzen in order to avoid a rock band and an unstable scree slope. After losing about 300m of height the path then tucks under an avalanche defence system with a projecting concrete lip to deflect falling stones. A series of short corrugated iron tunnels (no torch necessary) carries the route below the slope, before entering more larchwoods at the junction with the Täschgufer path (1940m, 2hr 30min).

TÄSCHALP (OTTAVAN, 2214M)

Also known as Ottavan, this hamlet lies at the junction of the Rotbach and Täschbach glens east of Täsch. There's a restaurant/touristenlager, an attractive little chapel, large cowsheds and a number of chalets. Upstream the Täschalpen pastures are drained by the Mellichbach stream which flows down from glaciers hanging below the Rimpfischhorn. On the hillside north of these pastures sits the Täsch Hut, with excellent views to the Schallihorn and Weisshorn, and from which a trail leads into the Rotbach glen to the north. Accessed from Täsch in the Mattertal by a winding service road, the Täschalp has a number of charming walks. (A twice-daily summer minibus service is available from the tourist information office opposite the station; 027 966 81 10, taesch@zermatt.ch. Taxis are also available.)

Accommodation and refreshments at Restaurant Täschalp-Ottovan (Europaweg Hut), 40 matratzenlager places, open June to mid-October (tel 027 967 23 01, **www.europaweghuette.ch**). Täschalp would be a good place to stay if you wish to split this long final day.

The confusingly named Europaweg Hut at Täschalp

A path descends from here to Täsch, while ours continues through the woods signed to Ottavan and Zermatt – watch for chamois as you wander through these woods. Rising among slopes carpeted with alpenrose and juniper the path emerges to a splendid view of the Matterhorn, then turns into the Täschbach valley, at the head of which stands the Rimpfischhorn. Eventually come down to a service road just below **Täschalp** (3hr 30min).

Walk up the road to a parking area just beyond the Europaweg Hut, then follow a path down to a footbridge over the Täschbach stream, signed Zermatt 3hr. Cross this and climb steeply to join a contouring path now heading north-west with a direct view of the Schalihorn and Weisshorn on the far side of the Mattertal.

Ignore alternative paths and curve round the hillside among larchwoods. After a short exposed section protected by cables, eventually reach a junction at a track hairpin bend. Take the left-hand fork and follow this uphill to a footpath junction where the Europaweg bears right.

As the trail progresses high above the Mattertal so views of Zermatt and the Matterhorn grow in extent. After 4.4km (approximately 2hr) reach a high point at 2350m, where the path levels out, before descending to meet a track at the alp hamlet of **Tufteren** (2214m, 5hr 25min, refreshments) and a choice of routes to Zermatt. The signed Europaweg path descends through the hamlet and straight down to Zermatt (1hr 15min). Other routes are also signed, while the preferred route via Sunnegga and Findeln is described below.

Turn left along the track leading to Sunnegga. On coming to a junction take the track rising ahead signed to Findeln, and before long reach another junction just below **Sunnegga** (2288m, 6hr refreshments). This area is badly scarred with bulldozed pistes and other trappings of the skiing industry, but only takes 15min to pass through. ▶

Follow the continuing tracks down, and after 15min (2.4km) a mountain café can be seen ahead. Take the descending track to the café (2114m), and then the narrow path that continues in the same direction just to the

For a fast and easy descent to Zermatt take the so-called Alpen-Metro 'Sunnegga Express' – an underground funicular – whose station is just above you near another restaurant.

right of the café, to join the main Winkelmatten path. Alternatively descend further to the village of **Findeln** (2051m, 6hr 15min, refreshments), a pretty little alp hamlet with several restaurants, a small white chapel and a classic view of the Matterhorn. Beyond this hamlet follow the Winkelmatten path, which gives good Matterhorn views almost all the way. It passes through more larchwoods, descending in long loops, crosses the Gornergrat railway and enters **Winkelmatten** (1672m, accommodation, refreshments), a 'suburb' of Zermatt, to which it is linked by electric bus. Turn right by the church and wander down to conclude the Chamonix to Zermatt Walker's Haute Route as you enter **Zermatt** (7hr).

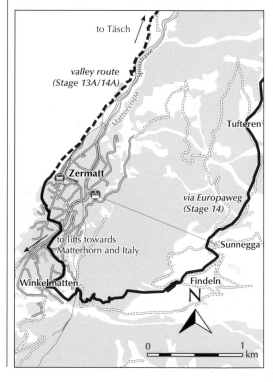

After Täschalp the Europaweg leaves the challenging sections behind (photo: Lesley Williams)

ZERMATT (1606M)

One of the great Alpine resorts, Zermatt's obvious success – in terms of popularity – is inextricably linked with the Matterhorn, whose noble presence overshadows the town and everything to do with it. But the Matterhorn is only one of many fine mountains visible, if not from Zermatt's crowded but traffic-free streets, certainly from the surrounding slopes. In fact there are more 4000m summits gathered round the head of the valley than are to be found anywhere else in the Alps. The appeal of the great snow and ice peaks remains as strong as ever to middle-ability mountaineers, while walkers of all persuasions will find sufficient scope here to fill every hour of a fortnight's holiday based in the town. But apart from outdoor activity and scenic splendour, Zermatt's sense of chic has as much to do with the expensive boulevards of Paris, Rome or London as it has with mountains. If you have a fortune to spend on glamorous fashion and jewellery, you might as well spend it here as in a polluted European capital. Then toast your latest accessory in champagne with the Matterhorn as a backdrop. Now that's decadent!

Accommodation, camping, restaurants, shops, banks, PTT, railway (to Visp, Brig, Geneva, etc). Tourist office, Bahnhofplatz, 3920 Zermatt (tel 027 966 81 00, **www.zermatt.ch**). There are more than 80 hotels listed within Zermatt itself, and many more on the outskirts. A free-phone booking facility will be found at the tourist office by the railway station. Lower-priced accommodation: Hotel Bahnhof, beds and matratzenlager (tel 027 967 24 06, **https://hotelbahnhof. com**); Matterhorn Hostel, matratzenlager (tel 027 968 19 19); Jugendherberge (youth hostel) in Winkelmatten (tel 027 967 23 20); Le Mazot (tel 027 966 06 06); Hotel Stockhorn (tel 027 967 17 47). The campsite is located just north of the railway station – functional, no frills, but well used by walkers and climbers.

225

STAGE 13A/14A
St Niklaus – Täsch – Zermatt

Start	St Niklaus (1127m)
Distance	23km
Total ascent	720m
Total descent	240m
Time	5hr 30min
High point	Zermatt (1606m)
Accommodation	Mattsand (40min): hotel; Herbriggen (1hr 10min): hotel; Randa (2hr 30min): hotel, pension, camping; Täsch (3hr 30min): hotels, camping; Zermatt: hotels, youth hostel, camping
Transport options	Train (St Niklaus–Zermatt)

Until the Europaweg was created (see Stages 13 and 14) this was taken as the final stage of the long walk from Chamonix to Zermatt, and although it has been eclipsed by that high and challenging trail, this valley walk will still be the preferred choice for those with limited time or as a bad-weather alternative. It is something of a tease, for naturally the Matterhorn is what you hope to see, but it remains hidden until the very end.

The walk, it must be said, is by no means the most scenic of the Haute Route for it never strays far from road or railway, and views are necessarily limited by the steep valley walls. However, it is not as uninteresting as you might fear, for there are hamlets and villages along the way, as well as ancient haybarns, meadows and forests – and the river, born of glaciers and great snowfields – that offer company along much of the route. Sadly, the entry into Zermatt by this route is an anti-climax, as the northern (downvalley) end of town below the railway station seems to be a permanent construction site. But at least the Matterhorn should make up for some of that.

An alternative finish to the trek if you only have one day available and wish to avoid the valley route described here would be to take a train to Täsch then walk or take a bus to Täschalp and walk to Zermatt from there. This is a highly recommended fine-weather option for those with limited time and is described below.

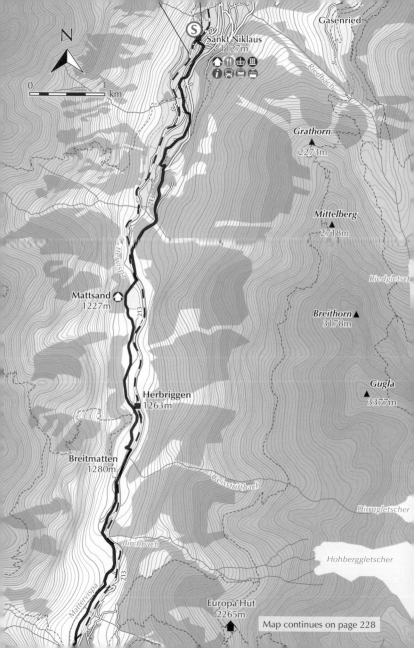

N

0 ___ 1 ___ km

S Sankt Niklaus
1127m

Grathorn
▲ 2273m

Mittelberg
▲ 2718m

Riedgletsch...

Mattsand
1227m

Breithorn ▲
3178m

Gugla
3377m

Herbriggen
1263m

Breitmatten
1280m

Geisstriftbach

Dirrugletscher

Birchbach

Hohberggletscher

Mattervispa

Europa Hut
2265m

Map continues on page 228

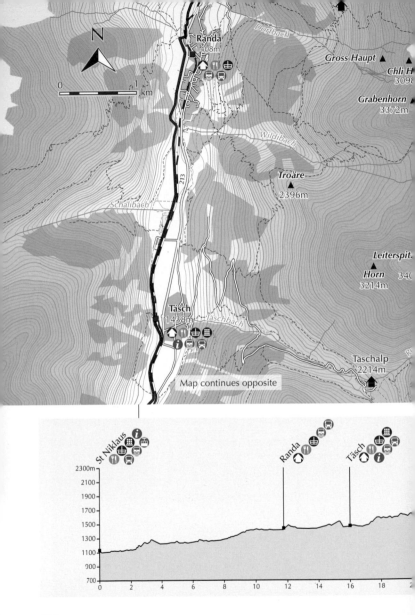

Map continues opposite

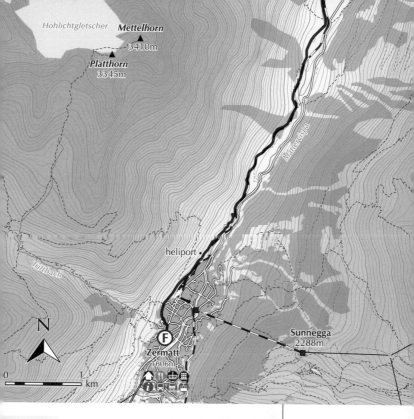

From the station, walk down to the village square and turn right, then immediately left down a narrow street to the old main road. Turn right and walk upvalley almost to the outskirts of the village (300 metres), where you turn to the right on a minor road 'Birchmatten' heading slightly uphill.

After 250 metres take a left fork on a minor no-through road signed 'Stahlen 46-104'. The road descends gently through meadows. After 10min when the road begins to rise take the small path on the left and descend to cross the footbridge over the Mattervispa river, then climb easily on the track which rises to join a minor road next to the main road. Continue up the valley for a further 10min on this minor road, passing chalets and other buildings. On coming to a second footbridge, take a small path on the left just before the footbridge, rising steeply through woods to join the main road. Turn right and follow the main road, and after a further 20min arrive in **Mattsand** (1227m, 40min, accommodation at Hotel zum Frävler, tel 027 956 27 07).

Join the old road and cross back over the railway line and the river beyond to gain a fine view of the Breithorn upvalley. The road now skirts a large settlement reservoir, and when the tarmac road bears left round the southern end, go directly ahead on a continuing track. About 1min along this track pass a small picnic area on the left, and on the right a view up to a series of cascades pouring through the Tummigbach gorge. Shortly after this emerge from a wooded area to open meadows and old haybarns, the village of Herbriggen across the river, and another lovely view of the Breithorn (1hr 20min).

THE BREITHORN

A near neighbour of the Matterhorn, the Breithorn is a massive snow and ice mountain of 4164m, with a 3km-long summit ridge. By its standard route (the SSW Flank) it is said to be one of the easiest of the alpine 4000ers to climb. But it also has some difficult and dangerous lines, especially on the North Face. It was first climbed (by today's *voie normale*) in 1813.

At the far end of the meadow the track forks, with the left branch crossing the river to **Herbriggen** (accommodation, refreshments). Continue upvalley along the right-hand side of the Mattervispa river, and after 15min (cumulative time 1hr 35min) come to a footbridge crossing the river to Herbriggen station. Again, do not cross, but remain on the west side of the river on a footpath signed to Randa, Täsch and Zermatt.

The path briefly accompanies the river then forks. Take the left-hand fork and continue next to the river until

On the valley walk to Zermatt, cascades can be seen pouring through the Tummigbach gorge

it briefly rises after 10min to a small cluster of chalets. Turn left and cross the bridge, then immediately turn right and follow the track as it gently rises next to the railway track (20min). Just ahead can be seen the results of a massive rockfall.

> In April 1991 a huge **rockfall** reshaped the mountainside north-west of Randa when a vast section of the Langenflueberg collapsed into the valley, demolishing the railway, blocking the river and cutting off the upper Mattertal for several days. Hundreds of large boulders still litter the valley where they came to rest in the meadows – close to chalets and haybarns – just below Randa.

Keeping company with the river the track continues upstream, then brings you to a service road by a bridge (20 min). Walk up the road, which bears right and rises steadily, screened from the river by larch trees. When the road forks, ignore the left turn and continue ahead on the rising track, with views now of the Weisshorn, with the icefall of the Bisgletscher just below it.

After just over 1km come to a road by a bridge on the outskirts of **Randa** (2hr 35min, 1408m, accommodation, refreshments, camping, trains to Zermatt) and take the right-hand road down towards a bridge and the railway. Cross both and turn left on a riverside

RANDA

Situated in the valley midway between the Weisshorn and the Dom, the attractive village of Randa is developing into a low-key alternative to Zermatt. It stands above the main Mattertal road and railway, so is relieved of through-traffic pressure. From the village a steep path climbs to the Europa Hut in 2hr 15min (see Stage 13) and the higher Dom Hut in 4hr. On the other side of the valley a 4hr 30min walk leads to the Weisshorn Hut. Apart from these lofty destinations, there are other good walks to be tackled from this valley base. The campsite, just to the south of Randa, has excellent facilities and views of the Zinalrothorn.

footpath signed to Täsch and Zermatt, which brings you to another junction 10min later. Remain on the tree-lined riverside path, now a track, which after a while rises through forest, then descends again to the river and forks. Cross the river to another service road, recross the river once more, then continue on the riverside path which goes up a brief slope, and leads to the Matterhorn Golf Course (2hr 35min).

With the river on your left and part of the golf course to your right, continue on the track by the river, pass beside a small man-made lake, at the far end of which you come to a large car- and coach-park.

Continue alongside the Mattervispa river, soon passing a picnic area with a water supply on the right. In 3hr come to Camping Alphubel opposite **Täsch** (1438m, 3hr 45min, accommodation, refreshments, shops, bank, PTT, trains to Zermatt). A bridge crosses the river to the village, but again, as with Randa, it is not necessary to cross unless you need its facilities. Instead, remain on the west bank of the river and 20min from the campsite you reach a group of barns where the way divides.

TÄSCH

Täsch is where the great majority of motoring visitors to Zermatt leave their vehicles before catching the train for the final leg of the journey upvalley. (Motor vehicles are banned from Zermatt.) The village used to be dominated by traffic and parking facilities but these have been very successfully moved underground and are well hidden from view, only the station remains visible. However, the original village stands aloof from all this on the west side of the valley, and is much more attractive and typically Valaisian in its architecture.

Behind it a steeply twisting service road climbs the hillside and enters the lovely, unspoilt Täschbach glen in which lies the hamlet of Täschalp, and above which stands the Täsch Hut. Access from Täsch can be obtained by using a twice-daily minibus service from the tourist information office opposite Täsch station (see details for Täschalp in Stage 14). There are some peaceful and scenic walks to be had up there, including sections of the Europaweg adopted by Stage 14.

This path is shared as a mountain-biking track for most of its way to Zermatt, so stay alert.

Continue ahead on a track (signed Zermatt 1hr 10min) which climbs next to the railway on the edge of larch-woods. The path stays close to the railway, and after a further 50min come to a high point to see the Matterhorn and Zermatt ahead. ◀

Climb past the heliport, then take the right-hand path fork to traverse the hillside. Finally the path passes behind large chalets and meets a road which continues down to arrive in the centre of **Zermatt** by the church (5hr 30min).

ZERMATT (1606M)

As one of the great Alpine resorts Zermatt has no real closed season. It's busy throughout the year – if not with skiers, walkers or climbers, then with the crowds of general tourists who flock there either to pay homage to the Matterhorn or to add the town to the tick-list of European hot-spots. Zermatt has something for everyone, and it's impossible to be bored there. If you don't like the crowds, there are paths that lead to magnificent viewpoints where even in the height of summer you can experience true solitude, and no shortage of other trails that, while not being empty, are well worth taking for their variety and extravagant panoramas. (See Appendix A for a sample.) If you're stuck in town on a wet day, why not visit the interesting Alpine Museum near the post office?

Accommodation, camping, restaurants, shops, banks, PTT, railway (to Visp, Brig, Geneva, etc). Tourist office, Bahnhofplatz, 3920 Zermatt (tel 027 966 81 00, **www.zermatt.ch**). For full accommodation information see the end of Stage 14.

Reluctant to finish the walk on our first Haute Route trek we sat on a bench on the outskirts of Zermatt. Since first light we'd had rain and knee-high clouds which somehow helped counter-balance all the fine-weather days. If views were to be denied us, this was definitely the day for it. Of course, that meant no Matterhorn, but what we had experienced in the previous two weeks more than made up for that loss. At Täsch the rain had stopped, but low clouds still obscured every view. Seated on the damp bench outside Zermatt we reviewed the walk as a whole, and concluded that it had been one of the most beautiful either of us had ever undertaken. (Between us we had more than 50 years of mountain experience.) Without doubt we'd be back to walk it again (as we have, several times). But for now we were in no hurry for it to be over. For all its undeniable attractions and for all its being the culmination of the walk that had begun on a sunny afternoon in Chamonix, Zermatt was not going to be another of those quiet, unassuming hamlets that had added so much to the route. We were about to face the crowds – and that would be a culture shock. So we sat among the clouds and put off the final ten-minute stroll into town. And we'd still be sitting there now had the rain not started once more.

Next day we were blessed with blue skies and sunshine, and so wandered upvalley with eyes transfixed by the sight of that great pyramid of rock. Our pilgrimage from Chamonix to Zermatt – Mont Blanc to the Matterhorn – was complete.

TÄSCHALP TO ZERMATT FINISH

For trekkers who only have one day to reach Zermatt but wish to take advantage of good weather and avoid the valley route, this finish seizes the great final balcony section of the Europaweg route into Zermatt, with the very best Matterhorn views. Either make a direct ascent to Täschalp from Täsch or take the twice-daily shuttle (early mornings and late afternoons). The full walk would be 17km, +1020m, -860m and takes 5hr 30min. If the shuttle is taken, the route from Täschalp takes 3hr 30min (13km, +250m, -860m).

Täsch to Täschalp: Turn south from the station and take the first road left alongside the culverted stream. At the small power plant at the end of the road pass between houses and begin the steep climb. Pass a prominent chapel and cross the road, passing abandoned farms. The first part of the climb is very steep. Thereafter the path levels out somewhat and crosses the road several times before arriving at Täschalp (2214m, 2hr).

Täschalp to Zermatt: Follow the route in Stage 14; 3hr 30min from Täschalp, 5hr 30min in total.

APPENDIX A
Walks from Zermatt

Zermatt

Should you have a day or two in hand on arrival in Zermatt and want to make the most of your time there, the handful of walks outlined below will provide some ideas. It is just a brief sample from the many to be had, but each one has its own special attributes and is highly recommended. Other ideas may be gleaned from the regional guidebook *Walking in the Valais* (Cicerone Press), which is readily available and is also usually on sale in Zermatt's main bookshop.

The Schönbiel Hut

This is one of the finest of all walks in the area giving a full day's outing – there and back. The path leads upvalley to Zmutt and beyond in full view of the Matterhorn. It takes you across glacial streams and along a moraine crest to the hut which is situated on a grassy bluff south-west of Zermatt, at 2694m, and with superb views onto a world of ice dominated by Dent d'Hérens and the Matterhorn. (4hr and 11km to the hut. Allow 6hr 30min for the round trip.)

Trift

The first part of this walk climbs through the confines of the Trift gorge immediately west of Zermatt, emerging to views of a glacier-hung cirque from the Victorian Hotel du Trift. From here you face several choices, but for the renowned belvedere viewpoint of Höhbalmen (2665m) a path is taken which crosses the Triftbach to the south and rises over grass slopes to turn a shoulder, beyond which you come to a wonderful broad pasture-land with a great sweep of mountains and glaciers in view. At a junction of paths you can either descend to Zermatt via the alp huts of Hubel and Herbrigg (a 4hr walk), or remain high on the continuing path that eventually descends into the Arben glen to join the Schönbiel Hut path (see the Schönbiel Hut walk, above). Bear left and return to Zermatt via Zmutt for a 7hr walk.

The Hörnli Hut

Situated at 3260m at the foot of the steep ridge on the Matterhorn from which it takes its name, the Hörnli Hut is where most climbers spend the night before embarking on the standard route to the summit. The hut enjoys a truly dramatic position overlooking a highway of ice leading to Monte Rosa. The walk from Zermatt is an extremely steep one (4hr 30min– 5hr), although the effort can be greatly reduced by taking the cablecar to Schwarzsee and beginning the walk there (2hr to the hut).

Fluhalp – four mountain tarns

For a less demanding day than any of the above walks, ride the underground funicular to Sunnegga at 2288m, descend a little, then take a signed path beyond the little Leisee tarn heading roughly east to the Stellisee and continue to the Berghütte Fluhalp (2607m), which is backed by moraines of the Findel glacier. Leaving the inn go down a track to a path serving the little Grindjisee, then continue by scenic track and footpath to the Grüensee. A short distance beyond this tarn stands the Bärghaus Grüensee near a path junction. The right-hand trail goes down to a footbridge over the Findelbach stream. Either walk down the left bank of the stream or cross over to the lovely alp hamlet of Findeln (visited on the final stage of the Europaweg) and descend from there to Zermatt (a 4hr 30min walk).

APPENDIX B
Climbing from Zermatt

Given time at the end of the Chamonix to Zermatt trek, and taking advantage of fitness, seasoned mountain walkers may be tempted to round off their trip by making the ascent of one of Zermatt's surrounding peaks. The Matterhorn is an obvious choice, but there are plenty of others. Experienced alpinists will need no advice from this book, but are directed to the two Alpine Club guidebooks to the area: *Valais Alps East* by Les Swindin and Peter Fleming, and *Valais Alps West* by Lindsay Griffin. The following notes, however, may be helpful for those with experience of climbing in Britain, but whose first visit to the Alps this is.

The first thing to understand is the scale of these mountains. After two weeks of wandering across their lower ridges you will have some idea of just how big they are, but it is only by setting out to climb them that the full stature of alpine mountains can be properly appreciated. They should never be underestimated. Unless you have a member of your party with all-round experience of climbing in the Alps, who is competent to lead a climb or two from here, my advice is to leave well alone or hire a professional guide.

Zermatt has its own mountain guide's office (the *Alpin Center*) with 50 or more official guides working

from it. The office is found on the main street south of the railway station (www.zermatt.ch/alpincenter). Guided excursions suitable for beginners are arranged daily, weather permitting. These include a 4hr glacier trek from the Klein Matterhorn to Trockener Steg, basic climbing instruction on the Riffelhorn, or the ascent of such 4000m peaks as the Allalinhorn and Weissmies.

A variety of other peaks can be offered, but it should be stressed that to employ a professional mountain guide here can be very expensive – although that expense may be justified by the knowledge that the experience of standing on top of your first alpine peak is likely to be one you'll always remember.

The cost of employing a guide for the climb itself is only part of the expense. Add to this the guide's food in a mountain hut (an overnight is usually necessary), hut fees for yourself and the guide, and hire of equipment – you'll no doubt need crampons, plus ice-axe – which can be rented from one of the many local sports shops. (The guide provides the rope.) It is also necessary to have mountain accident and rescue insurance.

The Mettelhorn
At 3406m this modest peak is not in the same league as those mentioned

below, but is a popular 'tourist' summit because of the extent and richness of its panorama. In times past an ascent of the Mettelhorn formed part of the training programme of mountaineers newly arrived in the area, for the 1800m difference in height from Zermatt to summit was considered ideal for acclimatisation and testing one's fitness! Having spent two weeks walking from Chamonix you ought to be fit by now, and the 6hr ascent by way of the Trift gorge, involving no technical difficulty, should be within the capabilities of most C–Z trekkers.

The Breithorn

Generally considered the easiest of the local 4000m summits (and possibly the easiest for its height in the Alps), the 4164m Breithorn is situated midway between Monte Rosa and the Matterhorn. The summit is reached from the Gandegg Hut via the Theodule Pass in about 4hr, while a shorter (1hr 30min) ascent of the SSW flank is often tackled from the Klein Matterhorn, graded PD-. The Breithorn is an extremely popular mountain, but given the serious nature of crevassed areas and the difficulties of route-finding in poor visibility, it should never be underestimated.

The Matterhorn

At 4478m this is possibly the one alpine peak all attracted to mountains would love to climb. The standard route by way of the Hörnli ridge is not difficult by alpine standards,

but is nevertheless a serious undertaking for novices, the rock being loose and downright dangerous in places. (The route is graded AD-, with numerous individual grade II and III rock pitches.) One of the problems faced by climbers on this route is salvos of stonefall; another, general to this mountain, is the bad weather it attracts. From the Hörnli Hut an average time to the summit for experienced climbers would be 5–6hr.

Monte Rosa

Containing the second highest summit in the Alps (the 4634m Dufourspitze) the Monte Rosa massif, which has no fewer than ten 4000m tops, is the largest mountain mass in Western Europe. Shared between Switzerland and Italy this beautiful snow- and ice-bound mountain boasts a number of lengthy routes. From the Monte Rosa Hut (see Appendix A) the Dufourspitze may be tackled by a popular snow climb up its north-west flank and then along the west ridge in 6–7hr (PD, II+ 40°). The first ascent was achieved in August 1855.

There are, of course, numerous other peaks in the area, many of which have routes of greater interest or challenge to experienced climbers. In addition there are glacier tours that would provide memorable days out. You need never run short of ideas in Zermatt.

APPENDIX C
Useful contacts

Tourist information
Switzerland Travel Centre Ltd
30 Bedford St
London
WC2E 9ED
tel 020 7420 4900/34
www.switzerlandtravelcentre.co.uk

Switzerland Tourism
608 Fifth Avenue
New York
NY 10020
tel 001 212 981 1177
www.myswitzerland.com

Valais Canton tourism and
accommodation information
www.valais.ch/en

Club Alpin Suisse
Monbijou str. 61
3000 Bern 23
tel +41 031 370 18 18
www.sac-cas.ch

Map suppliers
Swiss topographical maps can also
be ordered online from the Federal
Office of Topography in Switzerland
via www.swisstopo.ch

Edward Stanford Ltd
7 Mercer Walk
Covent Garden
London
WC2H 9FA
tel 0207 836 1321
www.stanfords.co.uk

Also: 29 Corn Street
Bristol
BS1 1HT
tel 0117 929 9666

The Map Shop
15 High St
Upton-upon-Severn
Worcs
WR8 0HJ
tel 0800 085 4080 (UK only)
tel 01684 593146
themapshop@btinternet.com
www.themapshop.co.uk

Cordee Ltd
www.cordee.co.uk

**Specialist mountain activities
insurance**
BMC Travel and Activity Insurance
(BMC members only)
177–179 Burton Road
Manchester
M20 2BB
tel 0161 445 6111
www.thebmc.co.uk/insurance

Austrian Alpine Club
Unit 43, Glenmore Business Park
Blackhill Road
Poole
BH16 6NL
tel 01929 556 870
https://aacuk.org.uk/
Membership of the AAC carries
accident and mountain rescue
insurance plus reciprocal-rights
reductions in SAC huts.

Snowcard Insurance Services
Lower Boddington
Daventry
Northants
NN11 6XZ
www.snowcard.co.uk

Geneva to Chamonix transfers
Cham-Van
tel +33 (0)1 75 43 01 32
www.cham-van.com

Mountain Drop-offs
Residence Lachenal
58 Allee Louis Lachenal
Chamonix
tel +44 (0)20 7043 4874
www.mountaindropoffs.com

The options at Tufteren (photo: Lesley Williams)

APPENDIX D
Bibliography

General tourist guides

The Rough Guide to Switzerland by Alice Park and Andrew Beattie (Rough Guides, 2017) – Entertaining, factual, full of surprises and highly recommended.

Switzerland by Gregor Clark, Kerry Christiani, Craig McLachlan, Benedict Walker (Lonely Planet, 9th edition 2018) – Good coverage, in typical Lonely Planet style.

Guides by DK, Bradt, Marco Polo, Berlitz, Michelin (and others) are also available.

Mountains and mountaineering

Numerous volumes devoted to mountaineering in regions of the Alps through which the Chamonix–Zermatt route travels are to be found in bookshops and libraries. Those listed below represent a very small selection, but there should be plenty of reading to provide an appetiser for a forthcoming visit – or to feed nostalgia. Please note that many of these older books are long out of print so only available through libraries and secondhand book specialists.

The Alps by RLG Irving (Batsford, 1939) – Long out of print, but available on special request from public libraries (it may also be obtainable via internet booksearch sites), this book contains lengthy chapters on both the Mont Blanc range and that of the Pennine Alps, with some interesting background information.

The High Mountains of the Alps by Helmut Dumler and Willi P Burkhardt (Diadem Books, London/The Mountaineers, Seattle 1994) – A sumptuous large-format book devoted to all the alpine 4000m peaks, of which there are many along the Haute Route. Mouth-watering photography and intelligent text make this a collector's item. (Out of print, available secondhand.)

Alps 4000 by Martin Moran (David & Charles, 1994) – This is the fascinating account of Moran's and Simon Jenkins's epic journey across all the 4000m summits of the Alps in one summer's frenetic activity. (Out of print, available secondhand.)

Scrambles Amongst the Alps by Edward Whymper (first edition 1871, numerous editions since, including one published in 1986 by Webb & Bower, with superb colour photos by John Cleare) – *Scrambles* is the classic volume of mountaineering literature which covers Whymper's alpine campaigns from 1860 to 1865. It contains the account of his fateful first ascent of the Matterhorn, but much more besides of interest to walkers of the Haute Route.

Wanderings Among the High Alps by Alfred Wills (Blackwell – latest edition 1937) – Another record of Victorian adventures with guides on peaks and passes of the Pennine Alps, as well as other areas.

The Alps in 1864 by AW Moore (Blackwell – latest edition 1939) – A two-volume personal account of a summer's mountaineering with Whymper and Horace Walker.

On High Hills by Geoffrey Winthrop Young (Methuen, 1927) – Winthrop Young was one of the great pre-First World War climbers whose accounts are of high literary merit. This volume includes many references to the Pennine Alps.

Men and the Matterhorn by Gaston Rébuffet (Kaye & Ward, 1973) – A well-illustrated book dedicated to the most famous mountain in Europe.

The Mountains of Switzerland by Herbert Maeder (George Allen & Unwin, 1968) – Large-format book with magnificent monochrome photographs.

Alpine Points of View by Kev Reynolds (Cicerone Press, 2004) – 101 full-page colour photographs, plus evocative text, that depicts the diverse landscapes of the alpine range – includes a number of images taken on the Walker's Haute Route.

The Outdoor Traveler's Guide to The Alps by Marcia R Lieberman (Stewart, Tabori & Chang, New York 1991) – Much of the range is covered, albeit in brief essays, but Mont Blanc and several of the Pennine valleys are treated well. The book is illustrated by Tim Thompson's high-quality colour photographs. (Out of print.)

Alpine Ski Tour by Robin Fedden (Putnam, 1956) – An account of the High Level Route ski traverse.

Mountain walking

Walking in the Valais by Kev Reynolds (Cicerone Press, 4th edition 2014) –
A walking guide in the same series as the present book, it covers all the
valleys of the Pennine Alps traversed on this route; 120 walks described.

Mont Blanc Walks by Hilary Sharp (Cicerone Press, 3rd edition 2016) –
A selection of 50 walks and four multi-day treks in the shadow of Mont Blanc
by a respected guidebook writer and trekking guide.

Tour of Mont Blanc by Kev Reynolds (Cicerone Press, 4th edition 2015) –
The early stages of the C–Z trek are shared by the TMB. This is the standard
guide to that classic trek.

100 Hut Walks in the Alps by Kev Reynolds (Cicerone Press, 3rd edition 2014) –
As the title suggests, a large selection of alpine hut walks. Some of those used
on the Chamonix–Zermatt route are included.

Classic Walks in the Alps by Kev Reynolds (Oxford Illustrated Press, 1991) –
A large-format book which describes, among others, the Chamonix–Zermatt
route plus several day walks in the Pennine Alps. (Out of print but available
secondhand)

Tour of the Matterhorn by Hilary Sharp (Cicerone Press, 2006) – A guide to this
'new' circular trek, which shares several stages of the C–Z route, but in the
opposite direction.

Tour of Monte Rosa by Hilary Sharp (Cicerone Press, 2015) – A guide to the
established TMR, which shares stages in the Mattertal with the C–Z route, then
climbs into Italy above Zermatt.

Trekking in the Alps edited by Kev Reynolds (Cicerone Press, 2011) –
The Chamonix to Zermatt route is included in a selection of the 20 best Alpine
treks.

The Swiss Alps by Kev Reynolds (Cicerone Press, 2012) – A resource for
independent adventurers planning to walk, trek or climb here, described in
detail valley by valley.

Walking in the Alps by Kev Reynolds (Cicerone Press, 2nd edition 2005) –
From the Alpes Maritime to the Julians of Slovenia, 19 regions of the Alps are

described with their walking and trekking potential in this 495-page alpine 'bible'. The Pennine Alps and Mont Blanc range are well covered.

Walking in the Alps by J Hubert Walker (Oliver and Boyd, 1951) – Inspiration for the previous title, Walker's book has long been out of print. Although much has changed in the Alps since it was written, it remains one of the best and most readable of all alpine books. A fine chapter is devoted to the Pennine Alps. (Available secondhand.)

Walking in the Alps by Helen Fairbairn, Gareth McCormack, Sandra Bardwell, Grant Dixon and Clem Lindenmayer (Lonely Planet, 2004) – A selection of multi-day tours and treks, includes the Walker's Haute Route. (Available secondhand.)

Walking in Switzerland by Clem Lindenmayer (Lonely Planet, 2nd edition 2001) – Good coverage of most Swiss mountain regions, in the Lonely Planet format. (Available secondhand.)

Backpacking in the Alps and Pyrenees by Showell Styles (Gollancz, 1976) – Contains an account of a large section of the Walker's Haute Route. (Available secondhand.)

Climbing and ski-touring guides

Valais Alps East by Les Swindin and Peter Fleming (Alpine Club, 1999) – A 'selected climbs' guidebook which includes many of the summits above Zermatt, but not the Matterhorn. (Out of print, available secondhand.)

Valais Alps West by Lindsay Griffin (Alpine Club, 1998) – Produced by that doyen of mountaineering journalists, this is the companion volume to the guide above. It covers most high peaks of the Pennine Alps from the Mont Vélan group to the Matterhorn. (Out of print, available secondhand.)

The Haute Route Chamonix–Zermatt by Peter Cliff (1993, Cordee) – Describes the glacier route for ski-tourers. (Out of print, available secondhand.)

Alpine Ski Mountaineering: Volume 1 – Western Alps by Bill O'Connor (Cicerone Press, 2002) – An inspirational guidebook to a number of terrific ski tours, it includes the Classic Haute Route, plus others in the Pennine Alps.

APPENDIX E
Glossary

The following glossary is a selection of words likely to be found on maps, in village streets or in foreign-language tourist information leaflets. It is no substitute for a pocket dictionary, but hopefully will be of some practical use.

French	English	German
French	English	*German*
accident	accident	*Unfall*
logement	accommodation	*Unterkunft*
selle	saddle, pass	*Sattel*
haut pâturage	alp	*Alp*
club alpin	alpine club	*Alpenverein*
florealpe	alpine flower	*Alpenblume*
avalanche	avalanche	*Lawine*
chambre d'hôte	B&B	*Hotel garni*
boulangerie	bakery	*Bäckerei*
chambres	bedrooms	*Zimmer/Schlafraum*
pont	bridge	*Brücke*
téléphérique	cablecar	*Drahtseilbahn, Seilbahn*
cairn	cairn	*Steinmann*
camping	campsite	*Zeltplatz*
château	castle	*Schloss*
télésiège	chairlift	*Sesselbahn*
chamois	chamois	*Gemse*
chapelle	chapel	*Kapelle*
église	church	*Kirche*
combe	combe, small valley	*Klumme*
salon	common room	*Gaststube*

French	English	German
crampons	crampons	*Steigeisen*
crête	crest, ridge	*Kamm*
crevasse	crevasse	*Gletscherspalte*
rimaye	crevasse between glacier and rock wall	*Bergschrund*
dangereaux	dangerous	*gefährlich*
dortoir	dormitory, simple accommodation	*Matratzenlager, Massenlager, Touristenlager*
est	east	*Ost*
facile	easy	*leicht*
brouillard	fog, low cloud, mist	*Nebel*
source, fontaine	spring	*Quelle*
sentier, chemin	footpath	*Fussweg*
sentier, chemin	footpath	*Wanderweg*
forêt, bois	forest	*Wald*
glacier	glacier	*Gletscher*
télécabine	gondola lift	*Gondelbahn*
ravin, gorge	gorge	*Schlucht*
bonjour	greetings	*Grüetzi*
épicerie	grocery	*Lebensmittel*
auberge	inn/guest house	*Gasthaus or gasthof*
randonneur	hillwalker	*Bergwanderer*
appartement de vacances	holiday apartment	*Ferienwohnung*
heure(s)	hour(s)	*Stunde(n)*
piolet	ice-axe	*Pickel*
renseignements	information	*Auskunft*
lac	lake, tarn	*See*
paysage	landscape	*Landschaft*
à gauche	left (direction)	*links*

French	English	German
carte	map	Karte
feuille	map sheet	Blatt
marmot	marmot	Murmeltier
moraine	moraine	Moräne
montagne	mountain	Berg
guide de montagne	mountain guide	Bergführer
cabane, refuge	mountain hut	Alphütte
hotel en haut	mountain inn	Berggasthaus
chemin de montagne	mountain path	Bergweg
alpiniste	mountaineer	Bergsteiger
chevreuil	roe deer	Reh
nord	north	Nord
col	pass	Bergpass, Pass
pâturage	pasture	Weide
sentier, chemin	path	Pfad
plaine or plan	plain	Ebene
gare	railway station	Bahnhof
gorge/ravin	ravine	Klamm
réservoir	reservoir	Stausee
arête	ridge	Grat
à droite	right (direction)	rechts
rocher	rock wall	Fels
corde	rope	Seil
sac à dos	rucksack	Rucksack
éboulis	scree	Geröllhalde
pension	simple hotel	Pension
pente	slope	Abhang
neige	snow	Schnee

French	English	German
sud	south	*Süd*
chute de pierres	stonefall	*Steinschlag*
ruisseau	stream, river	*Bach*
sommet, cime	summit, peak	*Gipfel*
torrent	torrent	*Wildbach*
office du tourisme	tourist office	*Verkehrsverein*
dessus	upper	*ober*
chambres libres	vacancies	*Zimmer frei*
vallée	valley	*Tal*
via, par-dessus	via, or over	*über*
belle vue	viewpoint	*Aussichtspunkt*
village	village	*Dorf*
eau	water	*Wasser*
ouest	west	*West*
ravin boisé	wooded ravine	*Tobel*
auberge de jeunesse	youth hostel	*Jugendherberge*

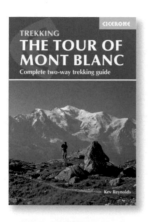

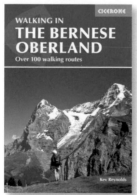
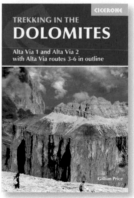

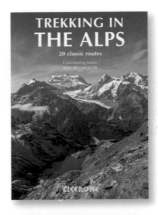

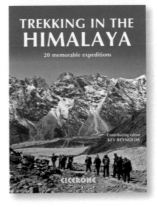

CICERONE

DOWNLOAD THE ROUTES
IN GPX FORMAT

All the routes in this guide are available for download from:

www.cicerone.co.uk/1048/GPX

as GPX files. You should be able to load them into most formats of mobile device, whether GPS or smartphone.

When you go to this link, you will be asked for your email address and where you purchased the guide, and have the option to subscribe to the Cicerone e-newsletter.

www.cicerone.co.uk

LISTING OF CICERONE GUIDES

DERBYSHIRE, PEAK DISTRICT AND MIDLANDS

Cycling in the Peak District
Dark Peak Walks
Scrambles in the Dark Peak
Walking in Derbyshire
White Peak Walks:
  The Northern Dales
White Peak Walks:
  The Southern Dales

SOUTHERN ENGLAND

20 Classic Sportive Rides in
  South East England
20 Classic Sportive Rides in
  South West England
Cycling in the Cotswolds
Mountain Biking on the
  North Downs
Mountain Biking on the
  South Downs
North Downs Way Map Booklet
South West Coast Path
  Map Booklet –
  Vol 1: Minehead to St Ives
South West Coast Path
  Map Booklet –
  Vol 2: St Ives to Plymouth
South West Coast Path
  Map Booklet –
  Vol 3: Plymouth to Poole
Suffolk Coast and Heath Walks
The Cotswold Way
The Cotswold Way Map Booklet
The Great Stones Way
The Kennet and Avon Canal
The Lea Valley Walk
The North Downs Way
The Peddars Way and Norfolk
  Coast path
The Pilgrims' Way
The Ridgeway Map Booklet
The Ridgeway National Trail
The South Downs Way
The South Downs Way Map Booklet
The South West Coast Path
The Thames Path
The Thames Path Map Booklet
The Two Moors Way
Two Moors Way Map Booklet
Walking Hampshire's Test Way
Walking in Cornwall
Walking in Essex
Walking in Kent
Walking in London
Walking in Norfolk
Walking in Sussex
Walking in the Chilterns
Walking in the Cotswolds
Walking in the Isles of Scilly
Walking in the New Forest
Walking in the North Wessex Downs

Walking in the Thames Valley
Walking on Dartmoor
Walking on Guernsey
Walking on Jersey
Walking on the Isle of Wight
Walking the Jurassic Coast
Walks in the South Downs
  National Park

BRITISH ISLES CHALLENGES, COLLECTIONS AND ACTIVITIES

The Book of the Bivvy
The Book of the Bothy
The C2C Cycle Route
The End to End Cycle Route
The Mountains of England and
  Wales: Vol 1 Wales
The Mountains of England and
  Wales: Vol 2 England
The National Trails
The UK's County Tops
Three Peaks, Ten Tors

ALPS CROSS-BORDER ROUTES

100 Hut Walks in the Alps
Across the Eastern Alps: E5
Alpine Ski Mountaineering
  Vol 1 – Western Alps
Alpine Ski Mountaineering
  Vol 2 – Central and Eastern Alps
Chamonix to Zermatt
The Karnischer Hohenweg
The Tour of the Bernina
Tour of Mont Blanc
Tour of Monte Rosa
Tour of the Matterhorn
Trail Running – Chamonix and the
  Mont Blanc region
Trekking in the Alps
Trekking in the Silvretta and
  Rätikon Alps
Trekking Munich to Venice
Walking in the Alps

PYRENEES AND FRANCE/SPAIN CROSS-BORDER ROUTES

The GR10 Trail
The GR11 Trail
The Pyrenean Haute Route
The Pyrenees
The Way of St James – Spain
Walks and Climbs in the Pyrenees

AUSTRIA

Innsbruck Mountain Adventures
The Adlerweg
Trekking in Austria's Hohe Tauern
Trekking in the Stubai Alps
Trekking in the Zillertal Alps
Walking in Austria

SWITZERLAND

Cycle Touring in Switzerland
Switzerland's Jura Crest Trail
The Swiss Alpine Pass Route –
  Via Alpina Route 1
The Swiss Alps
Tour of the Jungfrau Region
Walking in the Bernese Oberland
Walking in the Valais

FRANCE AND BELGIUM

Chamonix Mountain Adventures
Cycle Touring in France
Cycling London to Paris
Cycling the Canal de la Garonne
Cycling the Canal du Midi
Écrins National Park
Mont Blanc Walks
Mountain Adventures in
  the Maurienne
The GR20 Corsica
The GR5 Trail
The GR5 Trail – Vosges and Jura
The Grand Traverse of the
  Massif Central
The Loire Cycle Route
The Moselle Cycle Route
The River Rhone Cycle Route
The Robert Louis Stevenson Trail
The Way of St James – Le Puy
  to the Pyrenees
Tour of the Oisans: The GR54
Tour of the Queyras
Vanoise Ski Touring
Via Ferratas of the French Alps
Walking in Corsica
Walking in Provence – East
Walking in Provence – West
Walking in the Auvergne
Walking in the Briançonnais
Walking in the Cevennes
Walking in the Dordogne
Walking in the Haute Savoie: North
Walking in the Haute Savoie: South
Walks in the Cathar Region
The GR5 Trail – Benelux
  and Lorraine
Walking in the Ardennes

GERMANY

Hiking and Cycling in the
  Black Forest
The Danube Cycleway Vol 1
The Rhine Cycle Route
The Westweg
Walking in the Bavarian Alps

ICELAND AND GREENLAND

Trekking in Greenland –
  The Arctic Circle Trail
Walking and Trekking in Iceland

For full information on all our guides,
books and eBooks,
visit our website:
www.cicerone.co.uk

Walking – Trekking – Mountaineering – Climbing – Cycling

Over 40 years, Cicerone have built up an outstanding collection of over 300 guides, inspiring all sorts of amazing adventures.

Every guide comes from extensive exploration and research by our expert authors, all with a passion for their subjects. They are frequently praised, endorsed and used by clubs, instructors and outdoor organisations.

All our titles can now be bought as **e-books**, **ePubs** and **Kindle** files and we also have an online magazine – **Cicerone Extra** – with features to help cyclists, climbers, walkers and trekkers choose their next adventure, at home or abroad.

Our website shows any **new information** we've had in since a book was published. Please do let us know if you find anything has changed, so that we can publish the latest details. On our **website** you'll also find great ideas and lots of detailed information about what's inside every guide and you can buy **individual routes** from many of them online.

It's easy to keep in touch with what's going on at Cicerone by getting our monthly **free e-newsletter**, which is full of offers, competitions, up-to-date information and topical articles. You can subscribe on our home page and also follow us on **Facebook** and **Twitter** or dip into our **blog**.

Cicerone – the very best guides for exploring the world.

CICERONE

Juniper House, Murley Moss, Oxenholme Road, Kendal, Cumbria LA9 7RL
Tel: 015395 62069 info@cicerone.co.uk
www.cicerone.co.uk